# GIVE PEACE
TO MY SOUL

# GIVE PEACE TO MY SOUL

## DISCOVER ELIZABETH OF THE TRINITY'S SECRET OF PRAYER

*By Jean Lafrance*

BOOKS & MEDIA
Boston

Library of Congress Cataloging-in-Publication Data

Names: Lafrance, Jean, author. | Audette, Florestine, translator.
Title: Give peace to my soul : discover Elizabeth of the Trinity's secret of prayer / by Jean Lafrance ; translated by Florestine Audette.
Other titles: Apprendre à prier avec soeur Elisabeth de la Trinité. English
Description: Boston : Pauline Books & Media, [2018] | "Originally published as Learning to pray according to Elizabeth of the Trinity, by Jean Lafrance (c) 2003, Editions MediasPaul, 3965, Henri-Bourassa Boulevard Montreal, QC, H1H 1L1 Canada." | Includes bibliographical references.
Identifiers: LCCN 2018022568| ISBN 9780819831477 (pbk.) | ISBN 0819831476 (pbk.)
Subjects: LCSH: Elizabeth of the Trinity, Saint, 1880-1906. | Prayer--Catholic Church. | Contemplation.
Classification: LCC BX4705.E44 L3413 2018 | DDC 271/.97102--dc23

Originally published as *Learning to Pray According to Elizabeth of the Trinity*, by Jean Lafrance © 2003, Editions MediasPaul, 3965, Henri-Bourassa Boulevard Montreal, QC, H1H 1L1 Canada.

The original edition of this book has been edited and revised. The Preface was removed because it contained dated material that would not be relevant to a North American audience. Some adjustments to the chapter titles and subtitles have been made as well as other minor revisions to the language and content.

Éditions Médiaspaul thanks Canadian Heritage, The Canada Council for the Arts and SODEC (Société de développement des entreprises culturelles) for their support to the book publishing industry.

Translated by Florestine Audette

Cover design by Rosana Usselmann

Cover credit: istockphoto.com/© VIDOK

All rights reserved. No part of this book may be reproduced or transmitted in any form or by any means, electronic or mechanical, including photocopying, recording, or by any information storage and retrieval system, without permission in writing from the publisher.

"P" and PAULINE are registered trademarks of the Daughters of St. Paul.

Copyright © 2018, Daughters of St. Paul

Published by Pauline Books & Media, 50 Saint Paul's Avenue, Boston, MA 02130-3491

Printed in the U.S.A.

www.pauline.org

Pauline Books & Media is the publishing house of the Daughters of St. Paul, an international congregation of women religious serving the Church with the communications media.

1 2 3 4 5 6 7 8 9        22 21 20 19 18

# Contents

Foreword . . . . . . . . . . . . . . . . . . . . . . . . . . . . . . . . vii
Chronology . . . . . . . . . . . . . . . . . . . . . . . . . . . . . . . xi

INTRODUCTION
Elizabeth of the Trinity: A Teacher of Prayer . . . . . . . . . . . . 1

CHAPTER ONE
The Foundation of Prayer . . . . . . . . . . . . . . . . . . . . . . . . . 9
    Elizabeth's Trinitarian Focus . . . . . . . . . . . . . . . . . . . . . 11
    Loving Union with the Trinity . . . . . . . . . . . . . . . . . . . . 19

CHAPTER TWO
The Importance of Silent Recollection . . . . . . . . . . . . . . . . . 33

CHAPTER THREE
Aspects of Elizabeth's Prayer . . . . . . . . . . . . . . . . . . . . . . 49
    The Goal of Prayer . . . . . . . . . . . . . . . . . . . . . . . . . . . 51
    Simplicity in Prayer . . . . . . . . . . . . . . . . . . . . . . . . . . 55
    Rooted in the Word of God . . . . . . . . . . . . . . . . . . . . . . 62
    The Present Moment . . . . . . . . . . . . . . . . . . . . . . . . . 70
    In the Heart of the Church . . . . . . . . . . . . . . . . . . . . . . 78
    Mary: Model of Prayer . . . . . . . . . . . . . . . . . . . . . . . . 85

CHAPTER FOUR
Purification in Prayer . . . . . . . . . . . . . . . . . . . . . . . . . . . . . 89
    *Doctrine of Grace* . . . . . . . . . . . . . . . . . . . . . . . . . . . . . 91
    *Asceticism* . . . . . . . . . . . . . . . . . . . . . . . . . . . . . . . . . . 92
    *Methods and Result of Purification* . . . . . . . . . . . . . . . . . 94
    *Elizabeth's Dark Night* . . . . . . . . . . . . . . . . . . . . . . . . . 97

CHAPTER FIVE
The Christian Call to Intimacy with God . . . . . . . . . . . . . . 107

APPENDIX
Prayers to the Holy Spirit . . . . . . . . . . . . . . . . . . . . . . . . . 113

Notes . . . . . . . . . . . . . . . . . . . . . . . . . . . . . . . . . . . . . . . . 119

# Foreword

Today, more than ever, we need navigators of the spiritual life who can teach us to pray. The contemporary soul is not just spiritually empty—it suffers a ferocious vacuum as unrelenting winds of change and undercurrents of uncertainty threaten. Here the contemporary Catholic attempts to swim, but with little confidence that Church doctrine can fill this painful emptiness.

What we face today is not very different from what Saint Elizabeth of the Trinity, a young Carmelite nun, faced in early twentieth-century France. From the cloister, she helped her religious community and close friends navigate a hurricane of anti-religious bigotry and Church scandals even as she suffered the final stages of Addison's disease. To this day, she still draws souls out of themselves to help them to find those fair winds and following seas that lead to the bosom of Infinite Love.

The Carmelite family has been a special guardian of this mystery in the heart of the Church, providing no less than three Doctors of the Church and countless saints. Saint Elizabeth of the Trinity is perhaps the most influential of the twentieth century voices to join this chorus. The only saint born in the twentieth century whose spiritual writings are quoted in the *Catechism of the Catholic Church*, she has impacted devotion to the Father, Son, and Holy Spirit. Her writings and prayers have helped countless faithful to ponder the ultimate end of the Divine Economy: perfect unity with the Trinity. She helps us to see unity with God not as a future accomplishment but as a mystery that continually breaks into our lives in the present moment (see CCC no. 260).

By holding up Saint Elizabeth of the Trinity as a teacher of prayer, Father Jean Lafrance, a renowned priest of the diocese of Lille, France, effectively re-proposes the Catholic mystical tradition. Drawing from Saint Thomas Aquinas, Romano Guardini, Hans Urs von Balthasar, the Carmelite tradition, and many other spiritual writers, he provides the doctrinal context and practical advice in which Saint Elizabeth's clarion call to silence resounds. He draws us into her mission so that she might draw us into the shadow of the Holy Trinity.

When I was a student at the *Angelicum* in Rome, on a friend's recommendation I searched the Pauline Books and Media store near Saint Peter's for Father Jean LaFrance's classic work on Elizabeth of the Trinity. When I found it, the first few pages told me that Father LaFrance was just what I needed: a sure guide into Saint Elizabeth's wisdom and the mystery of living a contemplative life in the world. LaFrance's interpretation of Saint Elizabeth puts front and center the general loving awareness of the Lord's saving presence that our tradition calls mystical wisdom—a wisdom that animates all of the apostolic activity that the world needs today.

Years before, during lectures at Franciscan University of Steubenville, Dr. Mark Miravalle had revealed that then-recently-beatified Elizabeth of the Trinity, the mystic of Dijon, was an important influence on the spirituality of Saint John Paul II. That summer, while visiting the New Camaldolese Hermitage in Big Sur, I began to read her for the first time. When I first tasted her writings, I immediately hungered for more. Salted with the Sacred Scriptures and peppered with passages from the spiritual genius of the saints, real spiritual food is offered in her every sentence. A sense of validation shook my soul. At the same time, I also felt confounded and mystified.

The words were beautiful and compelling, but difficult to chew. My mind savored only a very small morsel of the feast being offered. To benefit from her message, I needed an introduction. Elizabeth of the Trinity invites one to dive into deep waters, but I needed someone to teach me to swim. She connects into a single whole the most sublime teachings, but without someone already acquainted with these truths, I struggled to apply them to life in a practical way.

That is why a fellow student in Rome recommended Father Jean LaFrance. His work was like a key that unlocked the door of my heart to friendship with Saint Elizabeth. In each chapter, he faithfully makes her focus his own: that of a transforming friendship with Christ, an immersion in the life of the Trinity, a fruitful union that heals, purifies, and intensifies human existence. For anyone who wants to grow in union with God and learn about this beloved saint, I highly recommend this classic work.

Originally published in 1963, *Apprendre à Prier avec Soeur Elisabeth de la Trinité* was among the first truly successful efforts to popularize Elizabeth's life and teachings beyond the Carmelite world. The work presents Saint Elizabeth within an accessible spiritual catechesis. This present edition offers a very readable and reliable translation. I truly hope that this work will continue to immerse those hungry for contemplative prayer in the spiritual mission of Elizabeth of the Trinity.

ANTHONY LILLES, S.T.D.
Saint John's Seminary, Camarillo
May 29, 2018

# Chronology

*July 18, 1880:* Elizabeth is born in a military camp of Avor in the district of Farges-en-Septaine, France. She is baptized four days later.

*October 2, 1887:* Elizabeth's father dies suddenly.

*April 19, 1891:* Elizabeth receives her First Communion and meets the prioress at the Carmel of Dijon. The prioress explains to her that her name means "House of God."

*June 8, 1891:* Elizabeth receives the sacrament of Confirmation.

*February 20, 1883:* Birth of Elizabeth's sister Marguerite.

*Summer of 1894:* After receiving Communion, Elizabeth hears the word "Carmel" in prayer. Her mother opposes the idea of her entering religious life. Elizabeth makes a private vow of virginity.

*1896:* Elizabeth visits Lourdes.

*1899:* Elizabeth reads *Story of a Soul* by Thérèse of Lisieux and *Way of Perfection* by Teresa of Ávila.

*March 26, 1899:* Elizabeth's mother agrees to allow her to enter Carmel.

*August 2, 1901:* Elizabeth enters the Carmel of Dijon, describing it as her "heaven on earth" (L 139).

*December 8, 1901:* Elizabeth is clothed as a novice.

*January 11, 1903:* Elizabeth's Solemn Profession.

*November 9, 1906:* Elizabeth dies of Addison's disease.

*November 25, 1984:* Elizabeth is beatified by Pope John Paul II.

*October 16, 2016:* Elizabeth is canonized by Pope Francis.

Her feast is celebrated on November 8.

INTRODUCTION

# Elizabeth of the Trinity: A Teacher of Prayer

In an age of scientific and technological discoveries, it is encouraging to see how many Christians show great interest in the spiritual life. The heart of every person harbors a desire for God that the external din and distraction of the world cannot dispel completely. Now is the time to help people to follow this desire for God through a rediscovery of the ways of prayer.

The Carmelite Order has a very special mission in our world: to teach the ways of contemplative prayer. The Carmel has always defined itself by its twofold mission in the Church. First, the invisible mission of silent mental prayer[1] is the very essence and center of contemplative Carmelite life; then, second, the visible mission testifies to a life hidden in God. The mission of Carmel is not to teach people methods of apostolic action, which is outside its scope. Rather, the Carmel reminds people of their greatest need: contemplation —without which a disciple cannot discover God at work in all of life's events.

The Carmel's timeless mission has a unique role in the twenty-first century. Busy and distracted, people in the modern world often hesitate to read the great spiritual masters. Today's readers are in such a rush, they imagine they can join the saints in their spiritual ascent without any preparation or detachment. In order to counteract this serious and risky illusion, God gives us the aid of spiritual guides whose mission is to direct us in the way of contemplative prayer. Among these guides, Saint Thérèse of Lisieux had a providential mission. Her autobiography, *The Story of a Soul*, is truly the bedside reading of souls yearning for God. In continuity with the mission of the Carmel, Thérèse penetrated in depth the essential message of Saint Teresa of Ávila and Saint John of the Cross. She cast her gaze on the All of God and now invites us to adopt her "Little Way" so we too may reach the summit of Mount Carmel—a feat that requires humility.

Saint Elizabeth of the Trinity had a similar mission. The little book *Souvenirs*, published in 1909,[2] continues to direct many persons to the decisive grace of intimacy with the Three Divine Persons. Elizabeth sensed her mission. A few days before her death, on October 28, 1906, she wrote to a friend:

> It seems to me that my mission in heaven will be to draw souls to an interior recollection by helping them to come out

of themselves and adhere to God in a very simple and completely loving movement. And to help them to stay in this great inner silence enables God to cast them in his image and to transform them into himself.[3]

Many have studied Elizabeth of the Trinity's spirituality. Perhaps most notably, the theologian and Dominican priest Marie-Michael Philipon gave her spiritual doctrine a theological structure. The great theologian Hans Urs von Balthasar also studied the writings of Elizabeth in order to present them in relation to current demands and aspirations.

On the fiftieth anniversary of her death (November 9, 1956), Father Anastasius of the Holy Rosary, Prior General of the Carmelites, defined Elizabeth's mission in the Carmel and in contemporary spirituality:

> Elizabeth is, in essence, a soul who understood and fully lived the ideal of our Order. It is impossible to consider this distinctive figure's thought in contemporary spirituality separately from her role as a Carmelite. . . . Her whole spirituality was nourished at the very heart of the Carmelite mystery. Her inner attitude was open to God; seeking God within, making a heaven interiorly, God's and her own heaven: there lies the dominant note of her whole inner life. Her quest for God, her openness, her orientation toward God and God alone is the essential attitude of the Carmel.

Since God has given us Elizabeth of the Trinity as a gifted spiritual guide in our time, we can go to her as disciples and ask her to teach us the art of prayer.

While Teresa of Ávila left us a complete teaching on prayer in her *Way of Perfection*, Elizabeth did not write long treatises on contemplative prayer. Yet in her writings we find many helpful suggestions for the necessary dispositions of a life of contemplative prayer, as Father Philipon explained:

> Elizabeth's mission was not doctrinal; she was never in charge of training novices in the practice of contemplative prayer. Her mission was chiefly one of life, prayer, silence, and suffering. Looking for a strongly systematized doctrine of prayer in her writings would therefore be in vain. Without claiming to fulfill the role of a theologian or a spiritual master, she was satisfied with living the great mystery of the divine indwelling as a contemplative. Elizabeth did not realize how her writings would be used in the future and did not even suspect that her doctrine would exercise a universal influence.[4]

For these reasons, Elizabeth's teachings are of great interest to those who are eager to become people of prayer. Too often, we speak of prayer as an activity apart from life, as if contemplative prayer does not have a deep bond with the rest of our existence. In reality, there is only one Christian life, and all of our spiritual efforts must tend toward the unification of the whole person. To the extent that we allow ourselves to become divinized,[5] our lives essentially become lives of faith, hope, and charity. Life becomes a continual prayer and our thoughts are united to the truth of God himself. We substitute God's point of view for our own, and charity transforms and divinizes our natural way of loving. Thus grafted onto the heart of God, people's hearts love God, the world, others, and themselves with a love that participates in God's love.

According to Elizabeth, it is necessary to cast our gaze on Christ, our divine model, in order to understand clearly the ideal unity between prayer and life. Jesus' attitude of complete dependence on the Father is the foundation of our prayer. Because Christ always fulfilled his Father's will, he lived in a perpetual state of offering and prayer. As Father Victor de la Vierge wrote:

> Jesus' perfectly unified life was entirely a prayer. His prayer was the expression of the bond that united Christ with his Father. The basic attitude of his being was to receive himself totally and constantly from the Father. The determining reason for the whole earthly, human, and divine existence of the Savior was the will to do and fulfill all that his Father wished and expected from him at every moment. Two living and praying were but one for him.[6]

In a similar but distant way, the same thing can be said about the prayer of Elizabeth of the Trinity. She was aware that her prayer was part of Christ's prayer, and this expressed her whole life in depth. In 1904, she wrote:

> Since Our Lord dwells in our souls, his prayer is ours. I want to be in constant communion with his prayer, taking my place like a small vessel at its source, at the fountain of life, so that I can then communicate it to souls, letting these torrents of infinite charity overflow.[7]

For this reason, we can go to Elizabeth of the Trinity—as we would to an older sister—so that she might teach us her spirit of prayer. But we cannot merely passively listen to her lesson, because prayer is a grace to ask for in humility and with perseverance. We do not read writings on the mystical life and contemplation simply to entertain ourselves with the discovery of a new world, and still less to form intellectual theories on prayer. Imagining we are praying is not praying.

The purpose of this book is to outline a useful teaching on prayer in the school of Elizabeth of the Trinity. All of the practical conclusions herein are not necessarily taken directly from Elizabeth's writings, but they are derived from reflections on them. The reflections will bear fruit inasmuch as they bring readers into true dialogue with the Lord. Without resolving to devote at least fifteen minutes each day to contemplative prayer, one's desire to pray is just a dream that won't have any real impact on life. Rather, prayer requires long and patient perseverance. Teresa of Ávila spent the first twenty years of her religious life in painful and arid contemplative prayer. Still, God never refuses the grace of prayer to the lowly and humble. One must never cease asking for this grace, even if one has to storm heaven to obtain it.

We need to understand Elizabeth's beautiful definitions of prayer in their vital context. Eight days after she entered the Carmel of Dijon, she defined contemplative prayer as follows: "The union of the one who is not with the One who is."[8]

But rather than focusing on how she defined prayer, it seems better to study her actions as a whole to help us to discover the deep source of her prayer in real life. Beyond her practical techniques and habits, we also will try to discuss what constituted her fundamental spiritual attitude in daily life. We will see that, like Christ, her prayer arose from a life of intimacy with the Father. Because her whole being was divinized, she made her life a continual contemplative prayer. During her last retreat before entering the Carmel, on January 23, 1900, she was already offering this prayer:

> Divine Master, may my life be a continual contemplative prayer; may nothing, nothing at all, distract me from you; neither my occupations, nor pleasures, nor suffering; may I be engulfed in you. Take my whole being, may Elizabeth disappear; may there remain only Jesus.[9]

We will attempt to enter this movement of contemplative prayer that was the theme of Elizabeth's entire life as a Carmelite. Elizabeth wrote that this movement was always united to an awareness of the Divine indwelling: "My whole exercise is to enter 'within' and to lose myself in those who are there. I feel God so alive in my soul; I only have to recollect myself to find him within me. This is what constitutes all my happiness."[10]

After looking at the heart of her fundamental attitude of prayer, we will then attempt to uncover the nature of Elizabeth's intimate dialogue with God. We will see that her life, hidden in God, required a radical death to every created thing. She came to full spiritual maturity only after a purifying night of trials. Then her soul was completely purified and she was prepared for transforming union with God. Having reached this summit, her prayer became an extension of Jesus' prayer. Elizabeth of the Trinity is, therefore, a model of prayer that every Christian may imitate.

CHAPTER ONE

# The Foundation of Prayer

Elizabeth of the Trinity's fundamental spiritual attitude was rooted in her prayer. In fact, the whole life of a Carmelite is focused on contemplative prayer. Pope Pius X once pointed out that Saint Teresa of Ávila's entire spiritual doctrine was basically one of contemplative prayer. Similarly, the exceptional value of Elizabeth's writings flows from her unique approach to the spiritual life, which implicitly teaches the stages of contemplative prayer.

We see in Elizabeth's writings the gradual growth of the life of grace that eventually took possession of her soul. However, at first this grace was only a seed that had to develop to its full potential. As grace took deeper root in Elizabeth's being, her spiritual life developed through her contemplative prayer. Like the fruit of a tree that grows as the sap feeds it, the more grace took possession of her soul, the more faith and charity grew in her.

In prayer, one enters within one's self to detect the first traces of those divine instincts grace puts there and to free them in an act of faith and love for God. Prayer remains difficult so long as these instincts are not fully developed so as to unite us completely to God. But, little by little, a life of intimacy with the Three Divine Persons gives an irresistible impulse to these instincts, and then life becomes a continual prayer.

We see this reality playing out in Elizabeth's life. The secret to her rapid growth in holiness was her awareness of the Divine indwelling in the most intimate center of her soul. She knew that a soul, sanctified by grace, is in God's presence. The Blessed Trinity was actively present in her soul, filling her with new life, drawing her more deeply into communion with God and participation in the mystery of Divine love. Before contemplating the mystery of the Blessed Trinity within her, however, Elizabeth was especially drawn to the contemplation of Jesus on the Cross. This orientation of her soul was evident in her prayer. Father Irénée Vallée[1] wrote of her:

> Her contemplative prayer was centered on the Crucified One for a long time. Then, she was attracted to the Blessed Trinity, to the need to belong to the "society" of the Father, the Word, and the Spirit. Everything became clear and more precise for her when she began to study Saint Paul.[2]

Elizabeth was seized by a love of the Divine Master and by a desire to be absorbed in contemplating his sorrows.

A significant fact reveals her spiritual focus before she became a Carmelite. She had hoped to receive the name Elizabeth of Jesus upon her entrance into the Carmel, because it reflected her desire for a transformation into the crucified Jesus—her ideal of holiness. Yet she reluctantly gave up this name when the Mother Prioress indicated she wanted Elizabeth to dedicate herself to the Trinity.[3]

A few days after she entered the Carmel, one of the sisters asked Elizabeth, "What is your favorite book?" She replied, "I don't have a favorite book. I prefer the soul of Christ, as it reveals all the secrets of the Father who is in heaven." Father Vallée further testified to Elizabeth's Christological attitude present from the very beginning of her vocation:

> It was a real joy to speak of Our Lord and of his grace with this soul who was so pure, so intuitive, and yet simple. She surrendered her will, as well as her intelligence, to her Master from the first moment of her vocation.[4]

## Elizabeth's Trinitarian Focus

Father Vallée greatly influenced Elizabeth's interior life by directing her to the mystery of the Divine indwelling in her soul, which would later become her vocation and mission. A particular grace to live this mystery was at the origin of her vocation. Father Philipon wrote that "God had given her the mission to bring souls within their inmost selves so that they might become aware of the divine riches of their baptism."[5]

At the age of thirteen, Elizabeth had received a mystical grace when she experienced a feeling of being "seized" by the Trinity. Imbued with the presence of God, Elizabeth felt at peace with these new experiences. Increasingly she immersed herself in a deep, silent recollection. Untroubled by her experience, she simply decided to ask her confessor to explain what was happening to her.

The religious environment of the Carmel favored the growth of this grace in Elizabeth. In the Carmel, living in the presence of God is a sacred legacy that dates back to the patriarch Elijah who once said, "As the Lord the God of Israel lives, before whom I stand" (1 Kgs 17:1). Elizabeth's diligent reading of Teresa of Ávila led her in the Carmelite way. On the first page of one of her notebooks, Elizabeth wrote this thought from Saint Teresa: "I must seek myself in you."[6] Once within the Carmel, Elizabeth soon learned that this awareness of God's presence is the foundation of the entire spiritual life. In Teresa of Ávila's commentary on the Our Father in the *Way of Perfection*, she notes that God is not only in heaven, "but in the innermost part of our soul," where we must know how to recollect ourselves in order to seek and find him. Teresa of Ávila also reveals that the goal of the mystical life is transforming union, or full and total intimacy with the Three Divine Persons. In the *Interior Castle*, she describes the Trinity as the summit of the mystical life. Souls that reach transforming union with the Trinity find blissful joys by living habitually in the presence of the Divine Persons.

Elizabeth found a complete spiritual doctrine in this Trinitarian insight that had become familiar in the Carmel. But, enamored with the truth, she desired to learn more. In 1902, Father Vallée preached a retreat at the Carmel of Dijon. This retreat helped Elizabeth to develop further the glimmer of insight she had glimpsed in the Carmelite tradition. Drawing on his experience as a contemplative theologian, Vallée spoke at length on the Christian dogma of Divine indwelling. His retreat helped Elizabeth to understand the theological foundation of her intuition. Vallée explained that God is present in us because he creates us at every moment. He used Saint Paul's text: "Do you not know that you are God's temple and that God's Spirit dwells in you?" (1 Cor 3:16), to show how, through baptismal grace, we become a spiritual temple. He taught that the Holy Spirit, along with the Father and the Son—who are inseparable from him—come and make their abode in us. This retreat reassured Elizabeth that she could confidently go within the depths of her soul, where she already felt so powerfully drawn.

From then on, Elizabeth was motivated by this fundamental spiritual attitude that provided a spiritual unification of her being. She would spend the rest of her life focusing on this insight and exploring its riches, growing in an ever-deeper life of intimacy with God. She wrote to a friend:

> Did I tell you my name in the Carmel is Marie-Elizabeth of the Trinity? To me, this name means a special vocation. I love this mystery of the Trinity so much. It is an abyss in which I

am lost. I am Elizabeth of the Trinity, that is, Elizabeth fading away, losing herself, letting herself be seized by the Three.[7]

This special vocation became the meaning of her life:

> This presence of God is so good! It is there, in my deepest self, in the heaven of my soul, that I love to find him, since he never leaves me. God in me, I in him, that is my life.[8]
>
> My happiness in life is the intimacy within, with the hosts of my soul.[9]

Before all else, the heart of Elizabeth's prayer is a contemplative prayer of intimacy with God. Because she abides in God, she experiences the need to express her adoration and love to him. For her, prayer is to stand in the presence of God within herself, to submit herself to God's loving influence, and to be attentive to the grace constantly active in her.

Like her spiritual mother, Teresa of Ávila, Elizabeth knew that Christ's humanity is the way that leads us to the Trinity. Finding God without going through Christ was never Elizabeth's model of prayer. On the contrary, she wanted to be transformed into Christ so that she could unite herself with his prayer:

> I no longer want to live my own life. I want to be transformed into Jesus Christ, so that my life may be more divine than human and so that when the Father bends over to see me, he might recognize the image of the "beloved Son in whom he was well pleased" (see Mt 3:17).[10]

Elizabeth expressed this in her prayer, "Elevation to the Blessed Trinity," which synthesizes her spiritual doctrine. Her only wish was to become an extension of Christ's humanity, thus responding to Saint Paul's desire: "In my flesh I am completing what is lacking in Christ's afflictions for the sake of his body, that is, the church" (Col 1:24). Through her identification with Christ, Elizabeth was united to the prayer, adoration, and love of Jesus for the Father. In her "Elevation to the Blessed Trinity" she wrote:

> O consuming Fire, Spirit of love, arise in me so that there may occur in my soul a sort of incarnation of the Word. May I be for Christ another humanity in which he renews his mystery.[11]

Though Elizabeth had a deep spiritual intuition of the Divine indwelling, she still had to discover how to begin living this reality in a concrete way, desiring this mystery to extend into her daily routine. Her prayer life began from this vital movement of her heart. One excerpt from her writings reveals the secret of her intimacy with the Lord:

> "Abide in me" (Jn 15:4). The Word of God is the one who gives this command, who expresses this will. Abide in me, not for a few moments, a few hours that pass by, but abide in me in a permanent and habitual way. Abide in me: pray in me, adore in me, love in me, suffer in me, work and act in me. Abide in me in your dealings with anyone and anything, always entering ever more deeply in me.[12]

Perhaps this excerpt best reveals Elizabeth's attitude toward her vocation in the heart of the Trinity. The word "abide" from the Gospel of John deeply impressed Elizabeth's loving soul, finding an immediate echo within her, a vibration that moved her entire being. The more one reads Elizabeth's writings, the more clearly one sees that she was a contemplative. This was her distinctive trait: she loved to *abide*, to remain in prayer before the Mystery that she loved. She gave her whole soul to God, and this is what Jesus loved in her, as he did in Mary Magdalene, whom Elizabeth admired. Jesus loves those who abide in him—and those who want to abide in him. He delights in those who find delight in him, and he tells us, "Abide in me . . . abide in my love" (Jn 15:4, 9). Hence, we have the Eucharistic promise with the same message: "Those who eat my flesh and drink my blood abide in me, and I in them" (Jn 6:56).

Before delving into methods of contemplative prayer, Elizabeth would want us to be aware of the basic attitude that keeps us constantly united to God. The only way to make a continual prayer of one's life is to abide in God and to live according to his holy will: "Father, I desire that those also, whom you have given me, may be with me where I am" (Jn 17:24). Elizabeth once commented on this passage:

> Such is Christ's last wish, his supreme prayer before he returns to his Father. He wants us to be there also where he is; not only during eternity, but already in time, which is eternity already begun. . . . The Trinity is our dwelling place, our "home," the Father's house, which we must never leave.[13]

Elizabeth's correspondence is filled with advice on living in God's presence. The same fundamental idea, adapted to different people and circumstances, always recurs in her writings: true life is found in the innermost depths of the soul with God.

Elizabeth was truly a soul with one idea. For her, holiness amounted to being closely united to the Trinity.[14] An intellectual discovery of this truth is insufficient, however. One must also thoroughly live this truth in order to become a soul of prayer. This truth can only be believed and discovered from within. To help us in this discovery, we can go back to Elizabeth's writings on prayer, allowing them to penetrate us, drop by drop, as dew into the soil. We must understand from within what abiding in Jesus Christ means. God calls all to this experience, but it is not solely the result of our human activity. It requires the direct help of the gifts of the Holy Spirit. In a letter to her mother, Elizabeth emphasized the need for this direct action of the Spirit in our soul:

> I am asking the Holy Spirit to reveal to you this presence of God in you of which I have spoken; you can believe my doctrine for it does not come only from me. If you read the gospel according to Saint John, you will see that at every moment the Divine Master insists on this commandment: "Abide in me and I in you" (Jn 15:4). And again, the beautiful thought that was at the beginning of my letter: "Those who love me ... my Father will love them, and we will come to them and make our home with them" (Jn 14:23).[15]

This life of intimacy with God, of which Elizabeth speaks, is a profound source of continual prayer flowing from the direct intervention and gifts of the Holy Spirit. Without the Holy Spirit's gifts, one can never become a person of authentic prayer.

Contemplative prayer must always start by calling on the Spirit's presence within us. As we begin times of prayer, we should not hesitate to spend five to ten minutes calling upon the Holy Spirit. It is impossible to pray without the help of the Holy Spirit: "No one can say 'Jesus is Lord' except by the Holy Spirit" (1 Cor 12:3). Gentle and respectful of our freedom, the Holy Spirit comes to us as One who purifies. Often we have a problem with prayer because we allow our egotism, impurity, self-interest, and self-love to dominate. We are so preoccupied with our perfection or imperfection that we forget the purpose of all true prayer: the glory of God and the establishment of his Kingdom here below. The Holy Spirit purifies our hearts by implanting charity in us: "God's love has been poured into our hearts through the Holy Spirit" (Rom 5:5). He purifies our minds by inspiring in us thoughts of God: "The Spirit searches everything, even the depths of God" (1 Cor 2:10). He purifies our wills by uniting our desires with the will of the Father: "All who are led by the Spirit of God are children of God" (Rom 8:14). The Holy Spirit comes to us especially as One who inspires. He teaches us how to act in union with God. He shapes our prayer by interceding in us with indescribable groans, urging us to cry out, "Abba, Father" (Gal 4:6). The Holy Spirit is a fire that burns in our hearts and keeps the love of God alive in us.

We can call upon the Holy Spirit with a very simple word or phrase. We can even call upon him without words, in a prayer that emerges from the heart and begs the Spirit to rise within us. We must not forget that the desire for God is already present in the innermost recesses of our heart. However, we may be unaware of this because our minds are so cluttered with worries and troubles. Therefore, we must free this desire. Father Vierge once described this desire for God:

> Relying on the desire for God is to rely on God himself. Saint Catherine of Siena taught that this desire, because it can grow infinitely, is able to reach God. God asks us to allow this profound desire that is born of God to grow and direct us to him.[16]

Sometimes, however, when we are feeling scattered, it is difficult to even recollect ourselves enough just to call upon the Holy Spirit. A busy life affects us and can make prayer an arduous task. When we do feel distracted, we can slowly recite the beautiful prayers *Veni Sancte Spiritus* and *Veni Creator* (see p. 116) to restore peace in our hearts. We may also use the prayer by Cardinal Mercier:

> O Holy Spirit, beloved of my soul, I adore you; enlighten me, guide me, comfort me, tell me what I ought to do, give me your commands: I promise to submit myself to all you wish from me and to accept everything you permit to happen to me. Let me know your will.[17]

## Loving Union with the Trinity

When Elizabeth was nearing her death, she wrote to a Carmelite sister: "It seems to me that I now perceive all things in the light of God, and if I began my life all over again, I would not want to waste a single moment."[18] Her mission, she wrote, was "to adhere to God by a simple and loving movement."[19] With her growth in the life of grace, sentiments of faith and charity defined her existence. She wrote that

> each minute is given to us so that we may become more and more rooted in God, according to the teaching of Saint Paul, so that our resemblance to the divine Model may be more striking and the union more intimate.[20]

Elizabeth grew to see all things not with her own eyes but with the eyes of Christ.

Elizabeth lived a life of intimacy with the Three Divine Persons through the virtue of faith. She journeyed for a long time through voids and periods of helplessness in prayer. Nevertheless, she remained a silent adorer of the God who was hidden in the center of her soul, as firm in her faith as if she were able to see the invisible God (see Heb 11:27). On certain days, the veil between Elizabeth and God seemed very opaque, but she refused to lose heart. She wrote to her sister:

> You must erase the word "discouragement" from your dictionary of love. The more you feel your weakness and experience difficulties in recollecting yourself, the more Our Lord seems hidden, the more you must rejoice; for then, you are giving to him.[21]

Nourished by the teaching of Saint John of the Cross, Elizabeth knew well that at the end of her life she would contemplate the unveiled Trinity, who was already her dwelling place here below. But as long as she was on earth, she had to move through faith to draw nearer to God. She wrote:

> Faith alone can shed true light on the One we love and our soul must choose it as the means to attain this blissful union. Faith pours all the torrents of spiritual blessings into the depths of our souls.[22]

Elizabeth lived this faith, and as her faith grew so too did her awareness of God's presence within her.

However, it is important to note that God's presence in Elizabeth's inmost self was not inert or unchanging. Rather, intimacy with the Divine Persons radiated through her whole existence. God's presence in her led Elizabeth to contemplate all things with the eyes of God. She described this interaction between faith and the presence of God in her soul:

> I place my faith in the presence of God, the God of all love, dwelling in our souls. I entrust everything to him. This inner intimacy with him is the beautiful sun that makes my life radiant and an anticipation of heaven.[23]

One reason many of us do not know how to pray is that we imagine God as distant or absent. How can we speak of intimacy in prayer if we see God in this way? We cannot be close to someone who is distant and is perpetually absent. For this reason, spiritual masters often advise those learning how to pray to settle firmly in the presence of God at the beginning of their contemplative prayer. If we spend the entire time of prayer time seeking God's presence, it is time well spent. We will certainly live in God's presence throughout the day.

Elizabeth also reminds us of a truth of prime importance: God is not far from us, he is very near, he is in us (see Acts 17:27). God's presence in the human heart inspired this beautiful prayer by Venerable Leonard Lessius:

> Lord, I beseech you, draw my heart to you, within my soul. There, far from the din of the world, far from the persistent worries that burden us, I remain close to you, take my delight in you, love you, venerate you, and hear your voice. There I will tell you the sadness of my life in exile! There, close to you, I will find the necessary consolations! Grant that I may never forget your presence in me, O light and sweetness of my soul! May I never forget you, but may the gaze of my soul meet you always and everywhere! You are everywhere, and all creatures are radiant with your presence. Just as our invisible soul manifests itself through the movements and operations of the body, so you also—who are the life of all that lives and the being of all that is—manifest yourself in the creatures through whom admirable wisdom and your almighty power shines.[24]

As this prayer illustrates, God dwells in us, works in us, and his presence requires a life of intimacy with him.

For Elizabeth, intimacy with God is not only a matter of staying in God's presence during times of prayer, but also of internalizing it throughout the day. She wrote:

> Living in the presence of God is a legacy that Saint Elijah left to the children of the Carmel. In the ardor of his faith, Elijah cried out: "As the LORD the God of Israel lives, before whom I stand" (1 Kgs 17:1). When Elijah heard the Lord approaching, he stood up and left the cave where he had

been hiding. Similarly, the soul must stand at the doorway in silent respect in the presence of God."[25]

As Elizabeth points out, Elijah's attitude is one of availability, like that of a servant who awaits his master's wishes. However, his attitude is not passive. Elizabeth expresses the attitude of the prophet Elijah when she speaks of living in God's presence. Indeed, Elijah stood in the Lord's presence to serve him. The expression "before whom I stand" in the passage from First Kings has also been translated as "before whom I serve." The prophet's stance of readiness before the Lord became action. Elijah was docile and responded promptly to God's commands. Father Philippe de la Trinité once described this stance before the Lord.

> Whoever stands in the presence of God does not do so to savor a blissful rest; but, vigilant, detached from all self-will, this person stands listening to God's designs of wisdom that are available in the religious fervor of the one who awaits a divine sign. An attentive vigil surrenders a person to God's desire, places him in God's hand to do with him whatever he wishes, to send him where he wishes. This person thus becomes the one who fulfills God's wishes: his servant.[26]

Elizabeth knew that living God's presence can be painful for our distracted nature. We often live superficially, skimming the surface of our being. Elizabeth believed it necessary to prayerfully ask for the gift of contemplation. She wrote:

> On the day of his feast we ask [Elijah] for the gift of contemplative prayer that is the essence of life in the Carmel, for

a heart-to-heart relationship that never ceases because, when we love, we no longer belong to ourselves, but to the beloved. We live more in him than in ourselves.[27]

At this point, we can review what Elizabeth of the Trinity has taught us thus far. First, Elizabeth's spirituality of prayer invites us to abide in God and to live continually united to him. Then, she teaches us that we do not have to go out of ourselves to find God. Rather, we need only enter within ourselves to live in the presence of the Divine Persons. Finally, Elizabeth teaches that it is possible to reach the summit of the spiritual life and to engage in an intimate and personal union with the Trinity. Love enables us take this decisive last step. Indeed, one's soul can always grow more in love and thereby immerse itself more deeply in God. John of the Cross described this process:

> When a soul, with all its strengths, knows God perfectly, loves, and enjoys him fully, it has reached the innermost center that is possible. Before coming to that stage, the soul is already well in God who is its center, but it is not in its deepest center because it can go further. Since love is what unites the soul to God, the more intense this love, the more deeply it enters into God and concentrates on him. . . . When the soul possesses only one degree of love, it is united to God through grace . . . but when this love reaches its perfection, the soul will penetrate its innermost center . . . until it is transformed to the point of becoming similar to God.[28]

In the Gospel of John, Christ describes the conditions for the indwelling of the Three Divine Persons: "Those who love me will keep my word, and my Father will love them, and we will come to them and make our home with them" (14:23). *Love* attracts and draws a person to God. It is not enough for us to possess God in the center of our soul; we must also live in fellowship with him (see 1 Jn 1:3). God is a consuming fire of love that conquers and transforms into itself everything it touches. Therefore, we can immerse ourselves in this burning source of love within the Trinity, which is the bond of the Father with his Word. We can enter this bond through faith and let ourselves be swept up in the movement of love that unites the Father to the Son. John of the Cross described this movement in *Spiritual Canticle*:

> The Holy Spirit with the strength of divine aspiration, raises and disposes the soul in a sublime way to breathe itself in God with the same breath of love as that of the Father in the Son and the Son in the Father, a breath that is this same Holy Spirit.[29]

We may try, but we cannot increase the love diffused in us by the Holy Spirit. Only God makes this growth happen.

Elizabeth describes God's action in the depths of the soul as "an enkindling of love in a mutual and eternal delight, a constant renewal in the bond of love."[30] God's action in our souls becomes evident when our natural way of loving is transformed. However, because sin turns us away from God, our wills do not have an immediate tendency to turn to God because sin directs us to sensory delights. Our love for God is always penitential. As long as the world draws us away from Divine union, we will need to be purified. The fire of Divine love consumes every hint of selfishness, impurity, and self-love in us. Christ made clear we are called to a love of conformity with the Divine will: "Those who love me will keep my word" (Jn 14:23). Elizabeth wrote: "The divine will must be our nourishment, our daily bread, we must sacrifice ourselves to all the Father wills."[31]

Drawn by the contemplation of the mystery of the Trinity in herself, Elizabeth submitted to God's action in her soul to the point of letting herself be filled completely by love. The remarkable grace she experienced crowned her entire life of love. She describes this grace in her spiritual biography:

> One morning, Elizabeth greeted her prioress in this way: "O Mother, a little longer, and you would not have found *Laudem Gloriae*[32] on earth. "How is that?" responded her prioress. "Last night, my soul was in a kind of helplessness, when suddenly I felt I was filled with Love. No expression can describe what I experienced; it was like a fire of infinite sweetness and, at the same time, it seemed to inflict a deadly wound on me. I think that if this had lasted longer, I would have collapsed."[33]

Here, Elizabeth speaks of a special grace resembling the wound of love described by Teresa of Ávila and John of the Cross (see *Living Flame of Love*, st. 1). On the feast of the Ascension 1906, God granted Elizabeth another special grace. That day, her prioress apologized for arriving late to the infirmary to visit her:

> "O Mother," the sick sister replied, "do not apologize; God gave me such a grace that I lost track of time. This morning,

I heard these words in the depths of my soul: 'If someone loves me, my Father will love him; we will come to him and make our dwelling in him' (see Jn 14:23). At that same moment, I saw how this was true. I cannot explain how the Three Divine Persons revealed themselves, but yet I could see them, holding their council of love in me, and it seems to me that I still see them. Oh! How great God is and how we are loved."[34]

By God's grace, Elizabeth progressed in the contemplative life so that she reached a point of transforming union with God. The Trinity took possession of her soul as a prelude to the union of love in heaven.

A few days before her death on November 1, 1906, Elizabeth gave her last testimony to the assembled community. She expressed her whole life in these words:

"Everything passes by! . . . At the twilight of life, love alone remains . . . We must do everything out of love; we must always forget ourselves: God loves it so much when we forget ourselves . . . Ah! If only I had always done so."[35]

Clearly, Elizabeth had fulfilled the desire she expressed soon after she had entered the Carmel: "I would like to die while loving, and thus fall into the arms of the one I love."[36] By focusing on love alone, Elizabeth's life became a continual prayer. We cannot understand her life of prayer apart from this movement of love that placed her in the heart of God. She once wrote to a friend:

Prayer is a time of rest, a moment of relaxation; we simply come to the one we love and stay very close to him like a little child in its mother's arms, and we let our heart go . . . There is only one occupation for a Carmelite sister: to love and to pray.[37]

The goal and foundation of Elizabeth's life was to love God, and this nourished her entire life of prayer. Teresa of Ávila, a Doctor of the Church, defined prayer as an exercise of love: "In my opinion, prayer is nothing else but being on terms of friendship with God, a frequent, intimate dialogue with him who loves us, as we know."[38] Prayer is a heart-to-heart relationship, a union and communion with God. If we find prayer difficult, an arduous task, it is often because we are speaking with Someone whom we feel is distant and to whom we give a little of our love, but not all our heart. To grow in prayer, we must enter a dialogue, a cordial conversation with God. We must allow ourselves to be confronted with the will of the Father.[39] In our dialogue with God, love must prevail. Of what use are our speeches or beautiful thoughts? We have nothing to teach God.

Consider a pleasant conversation between two friends. It has no useful, practical, or immediate purpose. When two friends meet, they simply share the best of themselves; they communicate to each another the riches of their hearts and minds. The quality of a conversation comes from the communion that occurs. Conversations with God in prayer should be the same. We come to contemplative prayer with the purpose of meeting Someone who is waiting for us, someone who wants to speak with us because he loves us. The first disposition of a prayerful soul is to wait on God: "Speak LORD, for your servant is listening" (1 Sm 3:9). Then we respond to God with the love he has already placed in our hearts. Even if we do not feel this love, we can tell God of our desire to love him and to abide with him throughout the day. Love needs no words and is content simply to remain in silence before the beloved. "What do you say to Jesus?" someone once asked Thérèse of Lisieux toward the end of her life. She responded, "I say nothing—I only love him!"[40]

When prayer feels tedious and boring, when we feel we have nothing to say and our heart is dry, go back to love. We can say, "Lord, I no longer feel the love I have for you, but I want to remain in faith near you and repeat my desire to love you, to be in communion with you." In matters of prayer, Father Étienne de Sainte-Marie reminds us:

> The primacy belongs to the will, as in matters of virtue the primacy belongs to charity. In the prayer of contemplation, Saint Teresa of Ávila recommends that we love more than we think in prayer. Prayer must be imbued through and through with love. Spiritual masters advise us to focus more on our affections rather than on our reasoning because, in this life, we cannot know God perfectly, but we can love him to perfection.[41]

Of course, we must never forget that to love God, we must first know him. But he also manifests himself to us in proportion to our love.

Elizabeth discovered her vocation and mission over time, but her search was focused. First, she probed the mystery of the Trinity in depth. This mystery became the truth that governed her entire life. Then, she discovered the fundamental attitude for her soul: to enter within herself, to remain in the presence of God's mystery, and to adore it. Elizabeth allowed herself be filled by the love of the Trinity—a consuming fire—until at the twilight of her life there was nothing but love.

To understand better this movement of irreversible grace that brought Elizabeth further within the Trinity, we turn to a prayer she composed two years before her death, a prayer that synthesized her spirituality.

## Elevation to the Blessed Trinity

> O my God, Trinity whom I adore, help me to forget myself completely and to establish myself in you, as still and at peace as if my soul were already in eternity. Let nothing disturb my peace nor draw me away from you, O my unchangeable One, but let every minute carry me further into the depths of your mystery!
>
> Give peace to my soul; make it your heaven, your beloved abode, and the place of your rest. Let me never leave you there alone; but keep me there totally present, completely vigilant in my faith, totally in adoration and wholly surrendered to your creative action.
>
> O my beloved Christ, crucified for love, I want to be the spouse of your heart. I long to cover you with glory, to love you . . . until I should die of love. . . . Yet

I feel helpless. I ask you to clothe me with yourself, to identify my soul with all the movements of your soul, to submerge me, to fill me, to substitute yourself for me, so that my life may be only a radiance of your life. Enter me as Adorer, as Redeemer, and as Savior.

O Eternal Word, utterance of my God, I want to spend my life listening to you, I want to become totally teachable so that I might learn everything from you. Through all darkness, all emptiness, and all helplessness, I want to be centered on you always and remain in your great light; O my beloved Star, make me so captivated that I no longer move away from your radiance.

O consuming Fire, Spirit of love, let it be done that an incarnation of the Word may occur again in my soul. May I be for him another humanity in whom he may renew his whole mystery. And you, O Father, incline yourself toward your little creature, see in her only the Beloved in whom you are well pleased.

O my "Three," my all, my beatitude, infinite Solitude, Immensity in which I lose myself, I surrender myself to you as your prey. Bury yourself in me so that I may bury myself in you, until I go to contemplate in your light the abyss of your grandeur.

November 21, 1904

CHAPTER TWO

# The Importance of Silent Recollection

If God abides in the center of the soul, asceticism should involve an effort of interiorization. The monks of the Eastern Church, according to the thought of Saint Augustine and Saint Teresa of Ávila, speak of a pilgrimage to the "place of the heart." But we know all too well that instead we often live on the surface, preoccupied with sensible impressions or with abstract reasoning. We may have to make a long journey to establish ourselves in the center of the soul where God is awaiting us. This journey can be made when we go beyond the senses and all that is created. As we do this we will progressively liberate our faculties and allow an encounter with God to happen in the dialogue of prayer.[1]

When Elizabeth of the Trinity entered Carmel, she found an entire tradition of prayer rooted in silence and solitude. For instance, the ancient *Rule of the Brothers of Mount Carmel* required Carmelites "to remain in their cell, in silence, day and night, to attend to prayer."[2] Reformers of the Carmelite Order, such as Saint Teresa of Ávila, made silence the first condition of the Carmelite life of prayer and union with God. Known for her skills as a conversationalist and her love of socializing, Teresa of Ávila heard these words from God that left a mark on her total conversion to holiness: "Henceforth, I no longer want you to converse with man but with angels."[3] Teresa of Ávila emphasized that to attain union with God a soul must be alone, pure, and burning with the desire to receive his grace. Saint John of the Cross also found silence at the very heart of the Trinity, and he wrote that the soul must remain in silence in order to be united to God. He alludes to the silence of the Trinity in his *Maxims and Counsels*: "The Father uttered only one Word, his Son, and this word he always speaks in an eternal silence. The soul must also hear it in silence."[4] These words echo the Book of Wisdom:

> For while gentle silence enveloped all things, and night in its swift course was now half gone, your all-powerful word leaped from heaven, from the royal throne, into the midst of the land that was doomed, a stern warrior carrying the sharp sword of your authentic command, and stood and filled all things with death. (18:14–16)

Imbued with the doctrine of her spiritual father, John of the Cross, Elizabeth discovered a model of silence in the silence of the Trinity. In one of her letters, she describes a "profound silence that arises in the soul, the echo of the one sung in the Blessed Trinity."[5]

To understand the importance Elizabeth gave to silent recollection in her spirituality, one must understand it in view of the Trinitarian life. Every time she speaks of prayer, Elizabeth relates it to union with God in the center of her soul. Reflecting one day on the mission she would fulfill in heaven she wrote:

> In heaven my mission will be to draw souls to an inner recollection by helping them to come out of themselves and adhere to God by a simple and loving movement. This great silence within allows God to imprint himself in them, to transform them into himself.[6]

Elizabeth knew that once she discovered the presence of God in herself, she would have to make a long pilgrimage to reach this divine presence. She never considered this process to be a negative aspect of her mission. She also did not turn away from noise to find a void in the silence. Rather, Elizabeth recollected herself in order to find a presence. Love drove her to silence: "For his sake I have suffered the loss of all things" (Phil 3:8). She wrote:

> Because of him, in order to adore God at all times, I am isolated, set apart, and detached from all things as much in the natural world as in the supernatural order with regard to the gifts of God. A soul that is not stripped of everything in this way, freed from itself, will necessarily be trivial and banal at times, something unworthy of a daughter of God, a bride of Christ, a temple of the Holy Spirit.[7]

Elizabeth's prayer life was a budding of grace that gradually took possession of her soul through the movements of grace. Her soul was fixed in God, who began his transfiguration by enlightening Elizabeth's intelligence through faith and inspiring her will through charity.

The more the Divine presence is imprinted on a soul, the more a person is filled with grace. Of course, growth in grace often meets many obstacles. In creating us, God established unity between the body and the soul, but sin breaks down his work. Sin breaks that original unity. Even if the unity between body and soul remains in a metaphysical sense, their harmonious unity is lost by sin. At the very least, the faculties of development are affected, argues a Dominican theologian, Father Bernard in his commentary on question five of Saint Thomas Aquinas' *De Malo*: "So, the result [of sin] is that nature will be less easily spiritual. But can we say that it is less human, that it has fallen below itself and is truly wounded?"[8] Sin introduces division into the soul; it alters the soul's relationships with God, with others, with itself, and with nature. This internal division is more profound and important than that between body and soul. Paul speaks of this division in his Letter to the Romans: "For we know that the law is spiritual; but I am of the flesh, sold into slavery under sin. I do not understand my own actions. For I do not do what I want, but I do the very thing I hate" (7:14–15). He also writes, "So I find it to be a law that when I want to do what is good, evil lies close at hand. For I delight in the law of God in my inmost self, but I see in my members another law at war with the law of my mind, making me captive to the law of sin that dwells in my members" (Rom 7:21–23). Sin leads us to lose full control over our faculties and senses. The imagination easily wanders, the intelligence focuses on merely human points of view, the will is weak, and the senses seek satisfaction outside the true good. Sin wounds our faculties and causes us to become divided and dispersed.

Grace works progressively to bring about greater integration. But grace requires our cooperation. The human will, moved by grace, must try to reestablish the total unity of being. For this reason, Elizabeth stresses the importance of silent recollection. For her, this includes the asceticism and purification spiritual authors have recommended in order to attain Divine union. Continual prayer, a life of union with God, is impossible without a healthy detachment from the senses and all that is created. In Elizabeth's writings, the word "recollection" extends beyond exterior and even interior silence. For Elizabeth, recollection extends to every effort of interior integration that fills a person with God's presence. The phrase, "movement of recollection," captures more accurately what Elizabeth intends to communicate. While she never used this expression, she does speak of a "simple and loving movement" that causes a soul to cling to God. She wants us to understand that a movement toward our innermost center is necessary in order to discover God's action within our souls.

We need to go within our hearts and recollect ourselves in silence in order to find unity in the midst of distractions, in the spirit of the psalm: "I hold my life in my hand continually, but I do not forget your law" (119:109). A unified person controls his or her senses and faculties, weaning them, so to speak, until they no longer ask for forbidden fruit: "I have calmed and quieted my soul, like a weaned child with its mother; my soul is like the weaned child that is with me" (Ps 131:2). As the movement of surrender characterizes Thérèse of Lisieux's spirituality, so the movement of recollection characterizes Elizabeth's spirituality. Recollection is essential to reach intimacy with the Three Divine Persons. As Saint Augustine wrote, "You were within me and I was seeking you outside of myself."[9] The Christian must reconstruct his or her interior unity around God's presence within.

Unfortunately, some interpret the counsels of Saint John of the Cross as suggesting that recollection is a process of negation or a denial of the senses. But that is far from true. Father Élie de Jésus-Marie writes:

> To recollect oneself is to assent to being, to allow various impressions to fall away and to remain before what is, in the present. The conversion realized by prayer is a movement of attention. Attention frees us from the multiplicity of life and turns our attention to the unique One. Through this positive unification, our attention establishes silence and opens the soul to the Presence. Far from culminating in a negation or a void, recollection results in plenitude.[10]

John of the Cross explained this process:

> When the spiritual person cannot meditate, let him learn to be still with a loving gaze on God, in quietness of mind, even

if he thinks he is doing nothing. Thus little by little—and soon—divine peace and repose will be infused into the soul with an admirable and sublime knowledge of God, wrapped in divine love.[11]

For Elizabeth, living in the presence of God requires simplicity and unity. In his writings on her spirituality, Hans Urs von Balthasar points out that for Elizabeth entering within oneself reestablishes the unity of the faculties in the act of existing and thereby unites us to God.[12] Elizabeth devoted the second day of her "Last Retreat"[13] to this subject. The text deserves to be quoted in full because it helps us to understand the heart of the movement of recollection:

> There is another song of Christ's that I would like to repeat constantly: "I will keep my strength for you" (see Ps 59:9). My Rule tells me: "Your strength will be in silence."[14] It seems to me that keeping one's strength for the Lord is to unify one's whole being through interior silence. It is to gather all our powers in order to put them solely toward the exercise of love; it is to have this simple gaze that allows the light of God to radiate from within us.
>
> A soul that argues with itself, that is concerned about its feelings, and pursues useless thoughts and desires, disperses its strength and is not completely directed to God.... There is still too much of the human element present. The soul withholds something within its inner kingdom, whose powers are not all "enclosed" in God, so it cannot be a perfect praise of Glory; it is not in the state of singing uninterruptedly the *canticum magnum*[15] of which Saint Paul speaks, because unity does not reign in it. And instead of persevering in its praise through all things in simplicity, it is

> constantly forced to adjust the strings of its instrument that are somewhat out of tune.
>
> How necessary this beautiful inner unity is for the soul that wants to live the life of the blessed here below, that is, of simple beings, of spirits. Is this not what the divine Master alluded to when he spoke to Mary Magdalene[16] of the *Unum necessarium*[17] (see Lk 10:42). How well the great saint understood this! Enlightened by the light of faith, she recognized her God under the guise of humanity and, in silence, in the unity of her powers, she listened to his words and she could sing: "My soul is always in my hands.[18]" [19]

Elizabeth's spirituality always returns to this movement of internalization and conversion. Some express concern that this pilgrimage of the heart could lead to excessive introversion or narcissism. But if one truly encounters God in this journey, there is no such danger. On the contrary, this process enables us to come out of ourselves and to leave behind self-centeredness in order to discover the will of God for ourselves and others.

Elizabeth often returned to her cherished theme of recollection. She always linked unity of being with a life of intimacy with God. She showed especially that we do not achieve this unity through stoicism, but in God who is the sole source of true unity. Elizabeth emphasizes this point in *Last Retreat*, her retreat notes. For example, she commented on Psalm 45:10–11 that has often inspired contemplative souls to leave everything behind and to seek the King's favor: "Hear O daughter, consider and incline your ear, forget your people and your father's house, and the king will desire your beauty." She writes:

This call is an invitation to silence, "Hear . . . incline your ear." But to hear, we must forget our "father's house," that is, everything related to natural life, this life of which the Apostle speaks when he says: *If you live according to the flesh, you will die* (Rom 8:13). To forget one's "people" is more difficult, it seems to me, because one's people is a part of us: it includes our feelings, memories, impressions, etc. in a word, the "self." We must forget it, leave it behind, and when the soul has severed those ties, when it is free of all that, "the King will desire your beauty," for beauty is unity, at least that of God.[20]

Elizabeth's message may seem intimidating to those immersed in temporal commitments and apostolic activities. How can we achieve such silent recollection when our duties pull us in so many directions and we have to face so many difficult situations? Finally, how can we find unity in the midst of the conflicting demands of daily life, when everything predisposes us to live merely on the surface?

First, let us affirm that the contemplative life can be lived in the midst of the world. We can aspire to a profound intimacy with God while living outside the cloister, without subjecting ourselves to the discipline proper to those dedicated to contemplative life. But if our goal is to live in true intimacy with God in our innermost hearts, then we cannot bypass the necessary means. In the sense that Elizabeth understood it, recollection is a necessary means to achieve union with God. Recollection is not a matter of retreating to a private cell and talking as little as possible. Rather, it is a basic disposition of a heart that can never rest except in God. External and internal noise, feelings, and judgments do not draw a recollected person away from their unity of being in God. Recollection makes it possible for those who have many contacts and pursue many commitments to remain always focused on God. Their actions are so purified that nothing distracts them from God. They also know the value of external silence because it is a condition for interior silence. Elizabeth was attentive to the reality that most people encounter, so her advice often applies to all ways of life: "What is this descent he is asking of us, if not an entering more deeply into our interior abyss? This act is not an external separation from exterior things, but a solitude of spirit, a liberation from all that is not God."[21]

Elizabeth emphasizes that recollection is not about an exterior separation from the world but a "solitude of spirit." Indeed, our movement toward the God within us requires the help of external things, including the people we meet. We should avoid an unhelpful opposition between our exterior and interior life.

Some people rightly feel uncomfortable upon hearing the expression "the interior life" for it can be synonymous with "escape." For this reason, perhaps it is better to speak of "the spiritual life." Recollection, therefore, is not an escape from the realities of life but involves being present to them in an enhanced way. The difference consists in how we accept the things of this world. For instance, we can welcome the people and events in our lives in different ways. We might welcome them in a superficial way that does not commit our entire being. Often we do this to satisfy our own emotional needs or our curiosity. When we act in this way, however, we do not express the profound unity of our being but allow events and people to erode it. These things become a "diversion" in Blaise Pascal's sense of the word.[22] But we can also encounter people and events with a sense of hospitality or acceptance that strengthens the unity of our being—choosing to accept or reject something through the litmus test of our faith. When we do this, we refocus on God.

An attitude of recollection can be especially difficult when we encounter people because our own masks and facades prevent us from meeting others on a deeper level, where their being is rooted in God. But if we manage to encounter people and situations in this way, then we have no reason to fear becoming unfocused. We can be fully present to another person or situation while remaining centered on God, whom we also encounter in the other person. This paradox can be expressed in these terms: The more we truly accept our deepest selves, the more enriched our being becomes. This attitude of truth is very demanding and requires great detachment, moving us beyond the realm of possessing to an ascent to the realm of being. People who want to make progress in the spiritual life must deny themselves everything, not out of a scorn for external things, but to possess them in their true being, which is united to God. John of the Cross advises: "Do not accept anything in your soul that has no spiritual substance, for it will make you lose your taste for true devotion and recollection."[23] When a person does this, John of the Cross insists that he or she is then rich and receives everything because he or she "no longer desires ... out of self-love."[24]

We need the help of grace in our effort at asceticism leading to the interior silence that makes prayer possible. *The Rule of Taizé*[25] defines this silence as follows:

> Interior silence requires, first of all, the forgetting of self in order to pacify discordant voices and to control obsessive worry, constantly beginning anew as a person who never loses heart because he is always forgiven. Interior silence makes conversation with Jesus Christ possible.[26]

In other words, unity of being is not a gift of nature we possess from the cradle but a goal realized over time. To accomplish this task, we must recollect ourselves in God, in the presence of Christ. *The Introduction to the Spiritual Retreat* by the Taizé community describes the benefits of this silence:

> In this silence so full of God, only things that are true and according to the will of God impose themselves on a person. Then one realizes that many cherished thoughts came from oneself and not from God, that many things must die, so that the New Self may grow.[27]

By keeping interior silence crystallized around the presence of God, contemplative prayer becomes easy and fruitful. Attention forms in us this interior crystal of which mystics speak, the crystal of pure prayer. Those who bear this crystal of silence in their inmost selves can lead the busiest of lives but their prayer and effective action will not exist in contradiction.[28] Interior silence must involve the whole being, all the faculties and senses. It quiets all useless thoughts and any subtle arguments that weaken the will and dry up love. It calms the imagination by weakening intense emotions, worries, and the din of vain thoughts. It purifies the memory by imposing silence on the past, especially on useless regrets and bitterness. It appeases the heart and the will by dampening unruly desires and hatred, excessive zeal, and exaggerated fervor. Silence enters heart's anguish and the soul's suffering. When one enters this interior silence, he or she enters self-forgetfulness. One no longer complains or seeks comforts. One is freed from selfishness. Interior silence is very useful in moments of temptation, especially when turbulent passions—such as self-centeredness, lust, indignation, vanity, jealousy, or resentment—assault or whirl around a person.[29]

When we feel overcome by such feelings, it is better to handle them gently rather than forcefully. One can use tact and discretion by suggesting to one's mind positive acts of humility and love of God. Perseverance and courage are the two great qualities required to bring peace to our souls when we are disturbed.

As noted, the movement of recollection is crucial for prayer because it establishes the soul in intimacy with God. Recollection allows a soul to be so transparent that it stays silent even in contemplative prayer. In a single act, often without words, it adores, offers itself to, and rests in God. This is the silence of eternity; it is the union of a person with God. Summarizing the thought of Dionysius,[30] Elizabeth points out that the silence the contemplative strives for resembles the silence of God:

> God . . . is the great Solitary One. My Master asks me to imitate this perfection, to render homage to him by being a great solitary person. Divinity lives in an eternal and immense solitude; he never comes out of it. All the while, he is interested in the needs of his creatures, for his solitude is nothing more than his divinity. . . . In order to guard against withdrawing from this beautiful inner silence it is necessary always to be in the same isolation, the same separation, the same detachment. My desires, my fears, my joys, or my grief—if all the movements coming from these four passions are not perfectly directed to God, I will not be a solitary soul, there will be disturbance in me; therefore calm, peacefulness of the powers, the unity of being are necessary.[31]

At first glance, it might seem paradoxical that Elizabeth, a mystic of the indwelling of the Three Persons, would benefit from Dionysius' ideas regarding the solitude of God. While Dionysius considers the Being of God and his autonomy of existence in the sense that God is incommunicable in his "ad intra" operations [that is, within the Trinity], Elizabeth uses the text in a more obvious sense. She sees the silence of the Trinity as the model and cause of her own interior silence, the silence that she desires to be made into "an echo of the one that is sung in the Trinity."[32] Elizabeth reiterates John of the Cross, who also exalted the silence of the Trinity: "The Father said but one word, that is his Son, and in an eternal silence, he always utters it. So must the soul hear it in silence."[33]

CHAPTER THREE

# Aspects of Elizabeth's Prayer

A few months before Elizabeth's death, one of her sisters gave a testimony that perfectly sums up the intense prayer life of this Carmelite of Dijon: "To me she appeared to be a personification of prayer."[1]

Elizabeth revealed her spirituality of prayer in her letters and other writings. She usually speaks of prayer in terms of a reality that has become natural to her. The presence of the Trinity filled her entire being to such an extent that prayer became the breath of her soul. She prayed as she breathed. Thus her sisters saw her as a personification of prayer.

We have thus far explored Elizabeth's reflections on prayer and shed light on several aspects of her prayer life. Our object is not simply to analyze Elizabeth's prayer but to learn how a soul totally given to God prays. For Elizabeth the source of prayer is God's grace along with the gradual training of our human faculties. She aims to know things not only from their appearances and from signs, but also through their nature and causes.[2]

To understand the nature of Elizabeth's prayer, we must look at its initial stages. Elizabeth entered Carmel above all to pray. At the age of fourteen, she wrote:

> I loved prayer a great deal, and God so much, that even before my First Communion, I did not understand how one could give his or her heart to anyone else; and from that moment on, I was determined to love God alone, to live only for him.[3]

At the age of ten, Elizabeth had glimpsed a truth that would gradually inform her entire life, leading her to become a person of authentic prayer. One can see the portrait of Elizabeth's life in her description of the Carmelite vocation:

> The Carmelite is a soul that has gazed upon the Divine Crucified One. She has seen him offering himself as a victim to the Father. Recollecting herself in this great vision of the charity of Christ, she understands his passionate love and wants to surrender herself as he did. On Mount Carmel, in silence, in solitude, in a contemplative prayer that never comes to an end and continues in the midst of all things, the Carmelite lives of God alone, as if she were already in heaven.[4]

The Carmelite strives to live heaven on earth. Knowing the significance of eternal life, Elizabeth wanted to make her life a never-ending contemplative prayer. She knew that heaven would be a place of continual praise and adoration, so she began her mission here on earth. She never separated her contemplative mission from her prayer of intercession. In anticipation of heaven, Elizabeth united her humble life to Christ who offered himself as a victim to redeem all. In heaven, Elizabeth continues to pursue her mission of intercession, as Thérèse of Lisieux, who promised before she died: "I will spend my heaven doing good on earth."[5] In a similar way, Elizabeth identified herself with Christ by becoming a soul of adoration and intercession.

## The Goal of Prayer

> What happiness it is to live in intimacy with God, when we make of our life a heart-to-heart relationship, an exchange of love with the Divine Master, when we know how to find him in the inmost depths of our soul. Then we are never alone again, and we need solitude to enjoy the presence of this adored Guest.[6]

When Elizabeth speaks of making one's life a heart-to-heart relationship with the Divine Master, she seems to echo Christ's call to "pray always and not to lose heart" (Lk 18:1). Elizabeth leads us to the goal of prayer: to make one's life a continual prayer. The means of prayer must always be considered in view of this goal.

As a Carmelite, Elizabeth was taught that prayer should gradually fill the entire day. From isolated acts, an attitude of uninterrupted prayer becomes an integral part of one's life. Elizabeth's life became an uninterrupted prayer on the day she felt seized by the Trinity at the age of thirteen. But before becoming an action, Elizabeth's prayer was an attitude of the soul that helped her to abide in God. She described her experience of continual prayer to a friend:

> I pray for you and keep you in my soul, very close to God, in this intimate sanctuary where I find him every hour of the day and night. I am never alone, Christ is always there, praying in me, and I praying with him.[7]

Elizabeth did not reach this stage of prayer through self-violence or force; she simply let time do its work. As twentieth-century theologian and priest Romano Guardini wrote:

> In the spiritual life, zeal is important but a lucid awareness that allows for time is just as important. When we understand that prayer is not an exceptional phenomenon, but a permanent element of existence, directed to God, we will seek to spread it to our whole existence.[8]

Though a life of continual prayer takes time, we should not become complacent. We need scheduled times of prayer. The Gospel depicts Jesus withdrawing from the crowd and going up the mountain to pray (see Mt 14:23, Lk 5:16). Through this behavior, Christ teaches us that fragile and distracted human nature needs moments of intense prayer to encounter the Father. We see the same thing on the psychological level. Continual prayer requires a loving attention; a constant desire to fulfill God's will at all times. Much like a spring that pools and slows the flow of water, we have to nourish this desire because it can get weaker throughout the day. Because our actions are not totally pure, when we pay attention to God we need to resist distractions. That is why we always have to purify our intentions and renew our desire to serve God.

The time we devote to contemplative prayer refocuses us on God and allows him to renew his dynamic presence within us, as the spiritual writer Father Léonce de Grandmaison wrote:

> Time particularly devoted to contemplative prayer is a means rather than a goal. Above all, it is the foundation of a life of prayer and a preparation for friendship with God. We all have experienced how daily life can be so secularized. This danger threatens everyone, and we fall into this temptation every time we no longer act in the presence of God and focus on the merely human and material level. The greater our union with God and our desire to please him, the more a supernatural spirit will imbue us. When this happens, our will grows stronger so that we may act purely in his service, as apostles, as divine instruments, and as friends of God. This spirit informs our lives, gives them character and value, and makes them pleasing to God. We become friends and servants of Christ, useful for the salvation of souls. The intense moments of our contemplative prayer imbue the fabric of our days with faith and charity. These moments place our lives in the will of God.[9]

Continual prayer is also not simply about being in a state of grace, and believing that in this state all our work offered to God is a continual prayer. Continual prayer is born from the desire of love. It exists when the will of God becomes our only love, and the glory and service of God our unique aspiration. We are imbued with spirit of prayer when we act for the sole motive of love and the glory of God. Saint Thomas Aquinas speaks of continual prayer when he writes: "Prayer ought to be continual: wherefore Augustine says . . . 'Faith, hope and charity are by themselves a prayer of continual longing.'"[10] Continual prayer exists when we have fervent charity and an impulse that inclines us to fulfill God's will at every moment. Our life's actions become true contemplative prayer when they unite us to God and allow us to savor the fruits of this union.

Prayer, as discussed earlier, is to unite oneself to God and to his will throughout the day. However, the will of God often remains merely theoretical for us. When the fabric of our lives is not fully imbued with faith and charity, we experience difficulty in adhering to God's will. The resolutions we make when we conclude a time of prayer are often too weak and imperfect to place us in total obedience to the Holy Spirit's inspiration. Father Jacques Loew[11] wrote: "Because we are human, we need an implement, a hinge by which the action of God is united to ours. This hinge is the present moment."[12] Elizabeth, too, often came back to this idea. She wanted to be in communion with God throughout the day, and she saw only one means to this: "[We must] surrender ourselves to love, busy ourselves in order to do the will of the one who first subjected himself to labor to provide us with an example."[13] God's presence in Elizabeth enlightened her gaze and strengthened her will so that she began to see him in all things. She wrote of her experience of continual prayer:

> The life of a Carmelite is a communion with God from morning to night and from night to morning. If He did not fill our cells and our cloisters, how empty they would be! But in everything we see him, for we carry him within us and our life is an anticipated heaven.[14]
>
> We find him in sleep as in contemplative prayer, since he is in everything, everywhere and always.[15]

For Elizabeth, the present moment and all the events of her life were like a sacrament of the presence of God.

## Simplicity in Prayer

Elizabeth certainly received special graces in contemplative prayer that helped her to reach a state of continual prayer. However, it would be inaccurate to think that she reached this stage without long effort. She must have dedicated herself to many moments of intense prayer so that she might journey through the ways of prayer. No one can aspire to continual prayer without imitating Christ, who often withdrew at night to pray. From a very young age, Elizabeth received the grace to withdraw in prayer. She would rise before dawn, even in the bitter cold, to enjoy an extra hour of prayer. Speaking of Elizabeth's prayer life before she entered the convent, the *Souvenirs* relates: "She received a spirit of prayer that kept her for hours in the church. One of her mother's friends asked her one day what she could be saying to God during all that time:

'Oh, Madam,' she replied, 'we love each other!'"[16] For Elizabeth, prayer was a true school of holiness.

Once she entered the Carmel, Elizabeth found a climate that fostered the development of her spirit of prayer. Everything was scheduled to encourage constant contact with God. Every day, the Carmelite devotes more than six and a half hours to prayer. Amid these moments of intense prayer, two hours are devoted to silent mental prayer—one at the beginning and one at the end of the day. Elizabeth, who yearned for prayer, found even this amount of time too short. She confided to a friend that between *Compline* and *Matins*,[17] she would spend another hour in prayer: "At a quarter to eight, *Compline*; then until *Matins*, which are said at nine, we pray. We leave the choir to retire to rest only at about eleven."[18] Elizabeth's schedule of prayer is astonishing and makes us reflect on the time we devote each day to contemplative prayer. Of course, those who are not living a monastic life cannot devote such long periods to daily prayer. For some, prolonged periods of prayer seem tedious, and it turns them away from prayer.

> Prudence is the virtue that rules every other moral virtue. Prudence knows how to manage times of prayer according to each person's vocation and the circumstances of his or her life. Saint Thomas Aquinas does not urge us to increase the time for prayer to the point of excessive weariness; it is virtuous to stop praying even if some other duty does not intervene.[19]

However, to foster mental prayer it is also necessary to spend enough time so that the soul can establish itself in a climate of silent recollection. Silence is necessary, for it creates within us a void that prepares us for prayer. This silence is actually not difficult; we simply need to keep quiet and listen to God.

Above all, prayer is a disposition of the heart that remains attentive to the Word of God. Too often, we think that prayer depends on us. We think we have to multiply our words and deeds in order to worship and love the Lord, as if we could somehow capture God with our actions. However, even before we pray, God is already at work, inspiring our hearts with movements of trust and love. In prayer, we rediscover this flow of divine life within us and allow it to rise actively to the surface of our awareness. Elizabeth once described what happens in these prayerful dialogues with God:

> Who could describe the sweetness of these heart-to-heart exchanges during which we no longer believe we are on earth; we see and hear only God. God speaking to the soul, God telling it such sweet things.[20]

Certainly not everything that comes up in prayer is necessarily a word from God. Generally, God does not speak to us in the same way a person would. Rather, he addresses us through events and especially through holy Scripture. We have to be attentive to the signs and secret movements the Lord causes to well up in us during prayer. Discernment helps us to recognize whether our insights come from ourselves or from the Holy Spirit. In a letter to a friend, Elizabeth once outlined in broad strokes the methods of her style of contemplative prayer:

> Ah, if you knew him a little, prayer would no longer bore you. To me, it seems to be a rest, a relaxation. We very simply come to the one we love, we stay close to him like a little child in its mother's arms and we let our heart go.[21]

Elizabeth's method of prayer does not constrain the spontaneous movements of the soul. Rather, for her, a prayerful heart merely stays close to God and remains united with him.

Mental prayer can be boring when we are not on familiar terms with God. We have little to say to someone we do not know and with whom we do not seek to enter into communion. On the other hand, conversation with a friend is inexhaustible. We do not know when to stop because there is so much to say to one another. Moreover, love sustains the conversation. At times, the dialogue may even be about trivial matters. Words seem inadequate to express fully the profound reality of what is in our hearts. No matter, the mere presence of a friend is enough to establish a warm conversation. Our dialogue with God is the same. The more we know him from within, the more time we find to devote to him in prayer. Then contemplative prayer truly becomes a moment of relaxation because we can confide all our concerns to the Lord.

During prayer, we stay in the presence of the One we love; we present to God our poverty and sin, and we ask him to be our holiness. But most of our time of prayer is devoted to love. First, we feel an affective love that calls for union. Then, as we conform ourselves to God's will, effective love extends to our entire life. If praying like this is difficult, we can try repeating an expression such as "Lord Jesus Christ, Son of the living God, have mercy on me," or "Jesus, meek and humble of heart, make my heart like yours." Little by little, these expressions of love will help us to enter into the rhythm of prayer, and the Holy Spirit will help us to savor each word from within. We also can try to slowly recite a well-known prayer, such as the Our Father, the Hail Mary, or a prayer from the Mass. When we do this, we can try to contemplate the realities behind words. Many spiritual writers agree that we should dwell leisurely on whatever point inspires us.

Contemplative prayer helps us to find the strength needed for the day, as Elizabeth once wrote:

> Our soul needs to draw its strength from prayer, especially contemplative prayer, in the intimate heart-to-heart relationship where the whole soul flows into God, while God flows into it to transform it into himself.[22]

According to testimonies, Elizabeth's mental prayer was always very simple. Her growing awareness of the presence of the Trinity in her soul was at the center of her prayer. All of her spiritual activity revolved around this intuition. She devoted much of her prayer to the loving contemplation of this truth, and then her prayer became a direct personal dialogue with the Lord.

Long before entering the Carmel, Elizabeth already was steeped in a simple form of contemplative prayer. Mother Marie de Jésus, foundress of the Carmel at Paray-le-Monial and then prioress at Dijon, testified to the simplicity of

Elizabeth's prayer when she described her visits to the convent before she entered:

> What should we say about the visits ... It goes without saying that we would speak of contemplative prayer: hers was very simple and straightforward. The Master was within, shaping her as he pleased. She protested that she did not do anything, ravished as she was by the one who was doing everything.[23]

Mother Marie de Jésus describes Elizabeth's very simple contemplative prayer, a prayer in which acts of the intelligence melt away into a single movement of loving knowledge that nourishes the soul.

Contemplative prayer involves many acts of love, while meditation involves reasoning as well. In contemplative prayer the intuition plays a greater role than discourse. In this kind of mental prayer, people often have the impression of doing nothing; but, in fact, their souls are much more active than they think. The supreme act of contemplation is a simple intuitive gaze that embraces all of reality in the same act. This prayer can become so simplified that the soul's only attitude is one of a silent gaze. Her retreat of 1904 was decisive in this sense for Elizabeth. The *Souvenirs* relates:

> Her contemplative prayer seemed to be still further simplified after this retreat: "We must look at him all the time," she said speaking of the Divine Master, "we must become silent, it is so simple." This was her only program.[24]

This prayer of simplicity generally involves some human activity, but it is a limited activity. In simple contemplation we remain the principal agent by means of our will with the help of grace, but in a higher degree of contemplative prayer our activity moves to another level and allows God to act. Spiritual authors call this prayer—in which God's activity predominates—a mystical or infused contemplative prayer. As a rule, the contemplative prayer of simplicity precedes infused contemplation. Simple contemplation predisposes us to a higher level of prayer, always leaving God free to grant his gifts as he sees fit for his glory and the good of the soul.

Elizabeth had a tentative knowledge of a higher infused state of prayer as described by Teresa of Ávila when she felt her soul completely seized by the Trinity. When she was eighteen years old, after a short retreat, she read the *Way of Perfection* by Teresa of Ávila and wrote:

> How I like the way [Teresa of Ávila] treats this subject when she speaks of contemplation, this degree of mental prayer in which God is the one who acts. He unites our soul so intimately with him that we are no longer the ones who live, but he is living in us ... I realized then what the master desired to grant me so often during this retreat (1899) and since. What can I give back for so many blessings? Ordinary prayer seems arduous and painful after these hours when the soul forgets everything and no longer sees anything but God. With what difficulty we must work to gather all our powers, how costly and difficult this is.[25]

It is important to remember that God freely gives these gifts and, after having granted this grace, he may withdraw it for long periods of time. He does so to purify the soul and to test the authenticity of its love. So, regardless of where we find ourselves in the spiritual life, we can imitate Elizabeth's attitude and return to prayer with patience in order to prepare ourselves for the gift of contemplation.

## Rooted in the Word of God

Before entering the Carmel and during her postulancy, prayer seems to have come rather easily for Elizabeth. But her years of novitiate were a time of darkness in prayer that purified and matured her faith and charity. She came out of this trial spiritually stronger and with her prayer more purified by the fire of love. She could say with the bride of the Song of Songs: "I am black and beautiful, O daughter of Jerusalem ... I am dark, because the sun has gazed on me" (1:5–6). God generally allows this way of purification for those he loves. He wants us to turn to him and so he often removes human assistance, leaving faith and charity as our sole guide.

During this dark night, Elizabeth's prayer began to center definitively on Holy Scripture as her way of going to God. The *Souvenirs* relates:

> Until then, the need to resort to the reading of our holy books had not been felt so much by [Elizabeth], who, in contemplative prayer, could drink in long draughts at the spring of living waters. But then, the meaning of the Holy Scriptures, especially of the admirable letters of Saint Paul, was truly given to her, as the luminous commentaries on the great Apostle interspersed in her correspondence testify.[26]

Elizabeth often cited Scripture in her correspondence and writings, seen especially in two of her last writings: "How to Find Heaven on Earth" (July 1906) and "Last Retreat of *Laudem Gloriae*." These writings seem to be commentaries on Scripture, reflecting on Saint John's Gospel and the Letters of Saint Paul. However, these writings are not mere commentaries. They reflect a continual discovery of her vocation as she was touched by the word of God. She experienced the word that is resolute in its brightness and that sheds light on each of our lives: "The word of God is a lamp to my feet and a light to my path" (Ps 119:105).

When Elizabeth offered herself to the word of God in contemplation, she felt God's gaze on her, and the movement of her Trinitarian life thus appeared as the will of God.

She became aware of God's initiative in calling her to be in communion with him through his word. "Beneath her apparent commentary on Holy Scripture," writes her biographer, "is hidden the secret of her holiness . . . her vocation fully realized in the twilight of her life."[27] The *Souvenirs* describes Elizabeth's experience of writing the "Last Retreat":

> She wrote these pages during painful periods of insomnia, in the grip of a pain so sharp that the poor child felt she was dying. They appear at first to be only simple reminiscences of her readings in Holy Scripture, accompanied by personal reflections. But they are more than that. One day, Elizabeth told her Mother Prioress that in this little book . . . she had tried to express how she viewed her office of praise of glory, how she understood that we could, even here below, live the

life of heaven. The dominant idea of her retreat was that of her whole religious life. "My soul is a heaven where I live while awaiting the Jerusalem of heaven," she wrote on the seventh day of her last retreat, "this heaven must sing the glory of the Eternal One, only the glory of the Eternal One."[28]

Elizabeth's constant prayer found substantial nourishment in Holy Scripture. She once wrote that the beautiful Letters of Saint Paul were her complete happiness.[29] She dwelt especially on the texts that shed light on her vocation as a Trinitarian soul.

As a true contemplative, Elizabeth centered on her mission at the heart of the Church: adoration. There she discovered her new name in Paul's letters: *Laudem Gloriae* or "Praise of Glory." Elizabeth wrote:

> The Apostle writes that '[God] destined us for adoption as his children through Jesus Christ, according to the good pleasure of his will, to the praise of his *glorious grace*' (Eph 1:5–6). There I found my vocation; since I will be praise of glory eternally, I want to be *Laudem Gloriae* already here on earth.[30]

Elizabeth instinctively discerned the permanent elements in her mission from the temporary. She knew that we are created to adore and serve God for all of eternity. In heaven, the elect "day and night without ceasing . . . sing 'Holy, holy, holy the Lord God the Almighty, who was and is and is to come' . . . [And they will] fall before the one who is seated on the throne and worship . . . they cast their crowns before the throne, singing, 'You are worthy, our Lord and God, to receive glory and honor and power'" (Rev 4:8–11). Elizabeth wanted to begin her eternal role here on earth and make her life a continual praise of God in adoration:

> In the heaven of her soul, the praise of glory already began her role for eternity; her song was uninterrupted for she was moved by the action of the Holy Spirit, who did everything in her. She was not always aware of this [action of the Holy Spirit]—for the weakness of her nature did not allow her to remain focused on God without distractions. But she always sang, she always adored. She was completely transformed into praise and love, in her love for the glory of her God.[31]

Praise was a central dimension of Elizabeth's prayer. Praise often escapes us for we lack a sense of the gratuitousness of God's grace. Contemplative prayer sustains our spiritual lives and enables us to entrust our intentions to God, but often we, rather than God, remain at the center of this dialogue.

> God is a jealous God: he wants to be sought for his own sake. He does not want to be simply a reservoir of energy for Christians who come to draw what they need to transform the world or simply to face the daily struggle of existence. Some Christians are astonished that they do not have a taste for God. This is undoubtedly because they do not seek God for his own sake, but for his blessings. God, at once all Other and very close, must be sought beyond what is useful, in the silence and solitude of the heart, where the gratuitousness of love and adoration finds its own reason.[32]

Many of us contemplate God at work in life events, but find it difficult to contemplate him through his word. However, to discover God in the events of life we must contemplate him in his divine deeds, in salvation history. The Lord's action in our life reflects the laws of divine pedagogy. The more we abandon our human views and enter into God's, the more we detect his work in our lives. This requires total detachment on our part and prolonged contemplation of God's action among his people.

If we find it difficult to adore God in our prayer, it may be we lack faith. Perhaps we do not believe strongly enough that God deserves to be contemplated and adored for his own sake. Our prayer may become easier if we consider our life on earth in light of heaven. In heaven, prayer is completely directed to praise and thanksgiving. So it makes sense to begin this contemplation now. If we do not take time to contemplate and adore God during our earthly journey, how will we be ready for the reality of eternity? The more we progress in our life of prayer, the more our contemplative prayer will resemble the prayer of the elect. Elizabeth always brings us back to this essential point. She avoids the nonessential in her doctrine of prayer and clings to what is lasting. Her message is similar to that of other contemplatives to the people of their own time.

Adoration is born within our hearts when we recognize we are creatures before God. Indeed, everything we have is from God: existence, life, health, talents, etc. We receive our being from God at every moment and the creative love of God sustains us in existence. In prayer, we must become aware of the bond of being—the source of our adoration—linking us with God. Moreover, we also receive supernatural existence from God. God gives us his grace at every moment and makes us his children. Prayer internalizes this bond of love, which is the basis of our thanksgiving. By giving thanks to God, we raise back toward God the divine life he has put in our hearts. As a homage of love, we return to him all the gifts and blessings we have received. Elizabeth describes the person who gives God this kind of praise:

> The "praise of glory" is someone who is always in an act of thanksgiving: each act and movement, each thought, aspiration, as they take root at greater depths in love, is like an echo of the eternal *Sanctus*.[33]

Seen in this perspective, adoration is not a fearful submission to a God who crushes us with his power, but our free and loving gratitude toward the One who constantly loves and creates us.

We cannot separate adoration from love; both call for and mutually fulfill each another. In prayer, we must hold both in balance: on the one hand, God's transcendence claims our respectful adoration; and on the other, God's presence in our innermost depths calls for our filial love. The contemplation of both aspects of God found in Scripture gives us a true sense of God. This is seen in the two great theophanies of the Old Testament: Isaiah's vision in the Temple (see Is 6:1–6) and Elijah's encounter with God at Horeb (see 1 Kgs 19:11–18).

Isaiah's vision places us in the presence of the thrice-holy God and calls for adoration and praise, while Elijah's encounter with God shows us a more personal God with whom we are called to be in a communion of love. Elizabeth helps us to enter deeply into these two aspects of the mystery of God. The eighth day of her "Last Retreat" has this reflection:

> Adoration, that is a word from heaven! It seems to me that we can define it as the ecstasy of love. It is love overwhelmed by beauty, the force, the vast grandeur of the Beloved. This love falls into a kind of weakness, a full and deep silence, the silence of which David spoke when he wrote: "Silence is your praise" (Ps 65:1). Yes, this is the most beautiful praise, since it is the one that is sung eternally in the heart of the silent Trinity; and it is also "the last effort of the overflowing soul that can no longer say anything."[34]

Elizabeth also used Scripture to shed light on her life. Especially in moments of trial or temptation, she drew strength from the word of God. As a true disciple of Saint John of the Cross, she never directly confronted suffering. Rather, she "slipped under" painful events or rose above them in order to surrender herself to the will of God as shown in the event. Saint Paul was also a guide in developing Elizabeth's spiritual orientation. She described how she dealt with suffering:

> I sought to rise above or to slip under it. I read Saint Paul who for me was always a means for grace; although faith was also required at those times, I assure you. I would reread my favorite passages, or I would ask my Master to lead me to the best pastures. And by ruminating on what I had thus found, I would overcome my troubles.[35]

Elizabeth shows us to the need for meditating on Scripture, preferably the Gospels, to nourish our prayer, drawing from it themes for our contemplation. It is helpful to choose the text we will meditate on in prayer the following day.

When we begin meditating on Scripture, it is good to read the text slowly, then to reread it several times, allowing the word of God to permeate us. Those with active imaginations might visualize themselves in the scene of a Gospel passage: entering into a dialogue with Christ, or trying to understand his feelings, his relationship with the Father, or his relationship with his disciples. Teresa of Ávila often meditated on a scene from Christ's agony or the scourging. It is good to devote time regularly to contemplate Christ's passion, a source of holiness and apostolic charity. We also might want to memorize a few Gospel passages so they can spontaneously come to mind during contemplative prayer. We might also try to incorporate some spiritual reading into our prayer. As a rule it is best to read little and slowly savor what is read and inspires us. Here are some helpful instructions for meditating on Scripture:

> During meditation, we must dwell on what enlightens and helps us to pray, without concern for anything else. Indeed, it is not a matter of meditating exhaustively on every aspect of a Gospel episode or of understanding it fully with the mind. The Gospel passage is simply a means for us to find Christ and to speak to him. Sometimes, a simple word in the text is enough. We may dwell on it without being preoccupied with anything else in the passage (one can always return to it some other time). Finally, if we do not feel inclined to speak to Our Lord and can only pray for several

minutes, saying nothing but only "savoring" Christ in a confused way, so to speak, and resting in his presence, so much the better. This is the most precious of prayers. It is enough to remain in prayer, even if we can only say a few simple invocations to Christ that we invent. For example, "Thank you Lord for making yourself known to me," or "Lord, you know that I want to love you," etc. . . . Saint Ignatius of Loyola, who was a master of prayer, once said that praying is to *gustare res interne*, or to savor the things of God interiorly. Ignatius gives this very important advice—when we reach the point of "tasting" something we are meditating on, we must not try to immediately move to something else. So, if we have reached an understanding of a particular word in a gospel episode and we feel that it enlightens us and does us good, then we should dwell on it and let go of any other distraction.[36]

## The Present Moment

Continual prayer, as already mentioned, helps us to act in charity, fulfilling the will of God at every moment. The gift we make of ourselves to God in contemplative prayer should also be expressed in the concrete dimensions of our lives. Otherwise, prayer is a pious fantasy. Wanting to be a contemplative without placing seeking the will of God is sheer nonsense. Our adoration of God must be proved by our deeds. Elizabeth writes:

> Let us adore him in spirit. Let us have our hearts and thoughts fixed on him, our minds full of his knowledge in the light of faith. Let us adore him in truth by our actions for it is above all by our actions that we show we are true; to do always what pleases God, the Father whose children we are.[37]

No one fulfills the will of God in a single act. As humans who live in time and space, we fulfill the will successively, over time. For us, word and deed do not always overlap. We do not always do what we say or say all that we do. Good intentions are not enough to keep us in a state of fervent charity, and the events of life often weaken the impulse of love that should enliven our actions. Moreover, we often live in a state of continual tension between the past and the future. We cling to the past and sometimes ruminate on past failures with regret. But life goes on, sweeping us along into the future. Sometimes we think we see happiness ahead: the joys of friendship or even union with God at the end of our efforts. But dwelling on the past or the future prevents us from living the present. Blaise Pascal was right when he wrote: "Let each one examine his thoughts, he will find them all preoccupied with the past and the future."[38] We can't step outside of time to resolve the tension, but we can establish balance, starting from real events and the people we meet. If we aim at escaping life by trying to unite ourselves with God apart from life's events, we go against God's will. He desires to be part of his people's history, especially through his Son and the events of his life.

Finding a balance in our prayer life helps us to be present to real life and the world around us. In order to do this, we simply forget the past and entrust it to the mercy of God. As Jesus said, "Let the dead bury their own dead" (Mt 8:22) and "No one who puts a hand to the plow and looks back is fit for the kingdom of God" (Lk 9:62). We also leave the future to

God's providence, knowing that he has foreseen everything for our good: "Therefore, do not worry, saying, 'What will we eat?' or 'What will we drink?' or 'What will we wear?' For it is the Gentiles who strive for all these things; and indeed your heavenly Father knows that you need all these things" (Mt 6:31–32). While we forget the past and entrust the future to God, we can be watchful not to isolate the present moment too much. Indeed, God is outside of time since he created it. He is the eternal present; at every moment he intervenes in history to sustain us in being and to give us his grace.

The great means to reach God is to meet him in the now, for God expresses his will in the present moment. God's will often takes flesh in the most trivial and minute details. Wherever the will of God is, God is present. In this sense, fidelity to the present moment places us in the continual presence of the Lord. That does not mean to isolate this moment, for our entire life is a continuation of each present moment.

> God awaits you in the present moment. If you agree to connect to it like a plug in the socket, light and strength will pass through to you. But in the vast space where you find yourself, there is only one socket, a small one, a very small one ... The present moment is the point of insertion where your life meets God, and through you, God enters the life of the world. But God does not come through you without your free consent.[39]

From contact with God in each moment is born a perpetual moment, a constant union with God through all things. While absorbed in active life, the contemplative soul dwells with Jesus in an unalterable moment of renewal, in a profound solitude with him alone. The contemplative can listen continually to the presence of God in each event and in every circumstance.

> The present moment is thus the very foundation of our union with God. To be sure, the divine presence shows through in prayer and in suffering. God is also present in the sacraments, in which God gives himself to us in a particular way. But every instant also gives us God. We could say that the present moment is in some way the perpetual sacrament.[40]

Thus, every moment of our lives is rich with eternity. Those who live in the present moment resolve the tension between the past and the future and the events around them do not crush them.

In the present moment, faith goes much further and helps us discover God at work. God's design of love brings us into being, and he has a plan for each one of us, a plan he wants to realize with our help. But he does not reveal this plan of love to us all at once. As he did with his Chosen People, God forms us through history, for each event of our lives is a moment of this history. If we look at our lives from a human perspective, we will see a succession of happy or sad events with no apparent connection. The gaze of faith, however, assures us that the great presence of God overshadows these events; through them, the Lord calls us to be in communion with his plan of love. To understand this truth better, imagine a stained-glass window of a Gospel scene. Imagine it with all of its separate pieces strewn about. We cannot guess the artist's intention when we see the stained-glass window in random pieces. However, if a diligent and expert artisan manages to restore the design by assembling the pieces, we can then discover the beauty, meaning, and harmony of the Gospel scene. Our life is like a stained-glass window whose artist and creator is God. Each event of our life is a piece of that stained-glass window. In order to understand its meaning, each part must be set in its proper place to reveal the overall design. Faith allows us to discover the plan of God beyond one event: "Each day is a gift of God; it is a present from God renewed with love which we must accept."[41]

Elizabeth had a magnificent understanding of the importance of the present moment. To help us discover its spiritual impact she wrote this about the soul that wants to live united with God:

> The divine good pleasure must be its nourishment, its daily bread. This soul must let itself be sacrificed to the will of the Father, in the image of his adored Christ. Every incident, every event, every suffering, as well as each joy, is a sacrament that gives God to us. Then the soul no longer sees any difference between these things; she lives them and rises above them to rest above all in her Master.[42]

By using the word "sacrament" in a broad sense, Elizabeth helps us to understand that a rich, hidden reality lies beneath appearances in life's events.

In a strict sense, the word sacrament is reserved for the visible signs chosen by Christ, signs that produce divine life in us by identifying us with Christ. Yet we know that the events of life are not altogether alien to the world of the sacrament. When God wanted to enter into a covenant with humanity, he usually did not intervene directly but used human mediums, such as people and events. In this sense, we can say that all of salvation history is sacramental, for God pours into it the riches of his divine life through effective signs. God's action is not tied only to the seven sacraments, for God reveals himself in many ways (see Heb 1:1–2). Father Ranquet wrote the following concerning this broader sense of the word "sacrament" so often used by Elizabeth:

> The sacrament is a constant in the divine plan; it is through people and events that God yields his invisible riches that he wants to give to humanity. Therefore, nothing new is here on the part of God. But on our part, there is a new attention with respect to the sacrament taken in its broad sense. In a strict sense, the Sacraments, it goes without saying, keep their richness and their prime importance. But, alas, they are not received often by many. . . . What leads to the Kingdom is not and cannot be its natural value: it is grace that moves in a hidden way in a measure known to God alone. . . . nature and grace, while being absolutely distinct, are not juxtaposed nor superimposed. They are composed, woven together, fitting into each other. While we see only a natural reality—because, in fact, this is what is seen—who knows if God our Savior, who journeys with us, is not in the process of making his grace pass through us in an invisible but authentic way? The Lord always uses the lowliest way: Israel, the Church, Nazareth, the Cross. The sacrament, properly speaking, is the rich means; the events of life are

the lowly way. In a manner that remains most humble and discreet in each case, both are channels of grace through which Christ wishes to irrigate all the areas of human life with his grace.[43]

Understood in this way, an event is not an accident that upsets our relationship with God, but a moment of God's design of love for us.

Everything that happens in life requires all of our attention on the human and the Christian level. First, on the human level, we consider the event in the objective and subjective aspects. In itself, what does this event mean? Is it positive or negative? What effect does it have on my intelligence, senses, and spiritual affectivity? In a word, what area of my being does this event touch? Did I accept it on the surface or in the depths of my being? "Did I lose myself in this event or did I consider it objectively?" We can also try to see how the event fits into our social and communal reality. Ultimately, this human view helps us to discover the constructive elements of God's action in us. Considered on the Christian level, the plan of faith can help us to see the authentic Christian values of the event. What is the Lord's call to me through this concrete situation? How can I meet him and unite myself to him?

Jean Pierre de Caussade often referred to what he called the "sacrament of the present moment":

> Divine life is given at every moment in an unknown but in a most certain way.... In this, faith finds its nourishment and support. It pierces through all, and clings to the hand of God who gives it life....

> God reveals himself to us in the most ordinary events of our lives, in a way as mysterious, but also just as real and worthy of adoration, as in the great events of history or of Holy Scripture. There is no moment when God does not present himself under the appearance of an event. Each thing is as a sacrament that gives us God.[44]

The gaze enlightened by faith can discern the presence of grace in each moment. If we lift the veil of human appearances, we can discover the face of God who calls us to union. De Caussade speaks of the "sacrament of the present moment" in this sense. God can act in us, inspire us, guide us, and enlighten us in the moment. He writes, "Clearly, if we could live in constant reference to the will of God, our whole life would be sacramental."[45] However, it is not enough to simply discover the will of God, for we also need to adhere to it in a movement of love.

Charity allows us to communicate with God's presence in the moment. Inspired by the spiritual teaching of Thérèse of Lisieux, Elizabeth viewed an attitude of surrender as the best expression of charity: surrender. Elizabeth once wrote to a friend on this theme:

> Surrender . . . that is what hands us over to God. I am very young, but it seems to me at times that I have really suffered at time. Oh! then, when everything became blurred, when the present was so painful and the future appeared still darker, I would close my eyes and surrender myself like a child into the arms of the Father who is in heaven.[46]

Therefore, we simply accept whatever happens as the expression of God's will by surrendering ourselves to his good pleasure. Passive surrender is very active for it requires the will to cling to what God wants for us. When the will of God is so internalized in our hearts, then it guides our will. The soul surrenders itself to God and allows him to act by removing all obstacles arising from sin. The soul recognizes the will of God by discerning it in each passing moment. Inasmuch as a person is faithful to the inspirations of the Holy Spirit, light will be more abundant in the future. Our response today conditions our response tomorrow. Our desire to always do the Lord's will Lord surfaces when we face events that bring us into constant prayer and, ultimately, contemplative life. This, and nothing else, is the secret to praying always.

## In the Heart of the Church

In her ardent desire to be in communion with the life of love of the Three Divine Persons, Elizabeth places herself directly in the heart of the Church's mystery. Throughout her writings, she rarely speaks of the link between the Trinity and the Church, yet she lived from this reality in her spiritual life and prayer. Without explicitly expressing this in theological concepts, she clearly senses the connection between these two mysteries. For this reason, she consecrated her entire Carmelite life to prayer and her sanctification for all souls, especially for the sanctification of priests.

By revealing the mystery of the Trinity—a communion of Three Divine Persons in the unity of one nature—Christ wanted to introduce his disciples into this life of love. We too are called to live in communion with the Blessed Trinity, to participate in the life of love that unites the Son to the Father. Throughout our pilgrimage on earth, we live this union in the obscurity of faith. One day, however, we pray that God's grace will bloom in glory and we will contemplate God face to face. But Christ does not want us to share intimacy with God in an isolated and individualistic way. He died so that all might be gathered together and that, together, we might be united to God. After the Last Supper, Christ asked the Father to unify all of humanity in the Trinity: "That they may all be one. As you, Father, are in me and I am in you, may they also be in us" (Jn 17:21). In this sense, we can say that the Trinity contains the Church and that she is its most fascinating image. Therefore, it is impossible to live in profound intimacy with the Three Divine Persons without desiring the union of all in this life of love. The Trinitarian vocation calls for and contains the ecclesial vocation.

Christ alone is able to bring about this union of all in the love of God. By offering himself to the Father as a victim, Christ won the forgiveness of our sins, and he infused divine life in us. Outside of Christ, salvation is not possible: "Apart from me you can do nothing" (Jn 15:5). We must firmly maintain this truth in order to understand our role in the redemption of the world. Christ does not want to save us without our participation; he gives us the honor of collaborating in our salvation. In a word, he gives us the grace to act so as to draw down graces on ourselves and for others. Christ communicates his grace to us at every moment through the intercession of his glorified humanity as the head of the members (see Eph 4:15) and as the vine for the branches (see Jn 15:5).

However, we are not inert instruments in God's work of sanctification. Our prayers, sacrifices, and good works collaborate in the growth of the grace in us completely won for us by Christ. The Council of Trent taught that the justice received [that is, grace] is preserved and even increased before God through good works.[47] The *Catechism of the Catholic Church* states that after we are given the initial grace of forgiveness and justification, "Moved by the Holy Spirit and by charity, *we can then merit* for ourselves and for others the graces needed for our sanctification, for the increase of grace and charity, and for the attainment of eternal life" (no. 2010).

In fact, the doctrine of the Communion of Saints allows us to go even further and affirm that we can also offer prayers and sacrifices so as to obtain graces for others. As Saint Paul wrote: "I am completing what is lacking in Christ's afflictions for the sake of his body, that is, the church" (Col 1:24). By the very fact that we are the members of a same body, the divine life circulating in us can water the rest of the body as well. Thomas Aquinas wrote on this subject, showing how all can be enriched from the holiness of the Church:

> Whoever lives in a state of charity, participates in all the good that is done in the entire world.[48]
>
> The work of the one who is with me in charity, in a certain way, is also mine.[49]

> What one seems to possess personally, is possessed by all in a certain way insofar as, through perfect charity, each considers the good of the other as his own.[50]

As a Carmelite, Elizabeth could not use exterior means of apostolic action to reach people and help them open up to divine life. Nonetheless, she, too, was called to labor for the growth of the Mystical Body.

The fruitfulness of Elizabeth's contemplative life found its origin and source in the interior means of prayer and sacrifice. By taking part in Christ's redeeming sacrifice, Elizabeth united her prayer to the One who "always lives to make intercession for them" (Heb 7:25). Saint John XXIII did not fail to stress the fruitfulness of such an existence. On the occasion of the Fourth Centenary of the Reformation of the Carmel, he recalled the great figure of Saint Teresa of Ávila. He emphasized how the Church—even at a time when the importance of external apostolic action was so pressing—still attributes the greatest importance to contemplation and continues to do so today, when external action is so emphasized. He wrote:

> Authentic apostolic action consists very precisely in participating in Christ's work of salvation. Now, this participation is impossible without an intense spirit of prayer and sacrifice. Christ redeemed the world, the slave of sin, mainly through his prayer and by sacrificing himself. So do souls who try to live this intimate aspect of Christ's mission, even if they devote themselves to no exterior activity, exercise an apostolic action in an eminent way.[51]

Elizabeth intensely lived this intimate aspect of her mission. While seeking to enter the intimacy of the Three Divine Persons, she made her own the feelings of Christ who offered himself to the Father for the salvation of all. Moreover, by her total detachment, she let Christ use her poor humanity to relive his redemptive mystery in her. Toward the end of her life, when her body was totally destroyed by disease, the thought of the salvation of others gave her great comfort.

By becoming a Trinitarian soul, Elizabeth broadened her soul to the dimensions of the Church, to the point that the interests of the Church became her own. In January 1906, she wrote:

> How we feel the need to sanctify ourselves, to forget ourselves and be totally absorbed by the interests of the Church. How sublime is the vocation of a Carmelite! She must be a mediator with Jesus Christ, to be for him an added humanity in which he can perpetuate his life of reparation, sacrifice, praise, and adoration.[52]

Elizabeth knew that prayer was the great means to take part in the redemption of the world, since prayer "wrests from heaven" the graces of conversion. We should not only be content with praying for this intention, but our lives ought to become a continual prayer. Prayer nourished by love is heard in the heart of God. She wrote:

> There is much to atone for, much to ask for. I believe that to respond to so many needs, we must become a continual prayer and love a great deal. The power of a soul surrendered to love is so great: [Mary of Bethany] is an example of

this; one word was enough for her to obtain Lazarus' resurrection.[53]

The prayer of the Christian opens his or her heart to the dimensions of the world. We need not be afraid to bring to God all the intentions of the Church. At first, we will feel an unavoidable tension between the prayer of adoration and the prayer of intercession. We may be under the impression that to implore God and ask him for graces is to remove something from the prayer of praise. However, we will soon understand that the glory of God and the salvation of souls are intimately linked. As we become aware of the poverty of our prayer, we will see how on our own we cannot give glory to God. Then we will beseech God to raise more souls of prayer and adoration throughout the world. We will also think of sinners, of the souls in purgatory, of persecuted Christians, of those who do not know God, and of those who suffer, and our intercession will become fervent for everyone.

Elizabeth knew her mission: to draw souls to great interior silence and to help them cling to God present within them. She prayed and sacrificed herself for this mission. This enabled her to awaken many souls in the world who would live in this great mystery of the Trinity. The vast scope of her mission had a resounding effect on souls. The striking example of one person who prays authentically is enough to awaken other souls to prayer. Few words are needed; but simply a great peace, recollection, and interior silence. We approach these people with respect because we sense in them a mysterious and perpetual dialogue with God. Their union with the Lord is reflected exteriorly by their joy and peace. We may wonder what motivates their attitude, and we eventually seek the cause in God. That is the great testimony of prayer.

In the Carmel, Elizabeth was a recollected religious. Those who observed her suspected that she was in a state of continual prayer. Two witnesses wrote:

> I will never forget the edification given to me by [Elizabeth] during a common retreat. The really touching piety with which I saw her make her Way of the Cross impressed me so strongly that I had more devotion contemplating her than in doing that exercise myself. Something irresistible held me in my place, simply united to her, and making her feelings my own to offer to Our Lord.[54]

> During the simple task of sweeping, she had an expression of profound seriousness and recollection on her face that would both strike and edify me at the same time. She seemed to be pursuing her constant praise through everything.[55]

Elizabeth also knew the art of seizing opportunities to say the right words to enlighten and encourage a person. On days when the nuns were permitted to visit each other in their cells and converse, the elderly sisters loved to talk with Elizabeth. They said that they received profound enlightenment from Elizabeth on their shared life in the Carmel. Her biographer wrote:

> Although she was very advanced in spiritual ways, this dear sister willingly made herself a disciple. One would have

thought that she had everything to learn. Because she was divinely instructed on contemplative prayer, I would see her listening with interest, deriving benefit from everything, without letting on that she knew a great deal more.[56]

Everyone who knew Elizabeth unanimously affirmed her spiritual radiance. She invited others to greater recollection and to self-sacrifice in order to love the Lord better. She is a model of contemplative prayer that we can follow. In prayer, spiritual knowledge is important, but nothing can replace a lived experience that introduces people to the life of prayer. People attentive to the present moment and who know how to discover the Lord's call can testify that opening the soul to prayer is always the beginning of authentic holiness.

## Mary: Model of Prayer

On several occasions, Elizabeth acknowledged the role of Mary in her life of prayer and recollection. She always had a devotion to the Blessed Virgin, but, in 1906, Mary began to influence Elizabeth's interior life in a definitive way. When Elizabeth began to experience suffering in her efforts in unifying herself to Christ, she ran to Mary, the Sorrowful Mother. During a pilgrimage to Lourdes in 1901, Elizabeth entrusted her vocation to Mary. It was around this time that Elizabeth began to call the Blessed Virgin *Ianua Caeli*.[57]

Elizabeth contemplated Mary's profound intimacy with God, especially how Mary lovingly received God's will, even when it was excruciatingly difficult. Mary was not scattered or distracted, but lived in constant dialogue with God. Elizabeth wrote: "The Queen of Virgins is also the Queen of Martyr; the sword will pierce her heart, for in her, everything took place within."[58]

Mary is truly the model of contemplative souls. All the movements of her heart were ordered according to the fulfillment of God's will. She united herself to God—who is Love—living within her. Elizabeth wrote that Mary's soul was so simple that "she seemed to reproduce on earth the life of the Divine Being, the simple Being."[59] Aware of the fullness of grace that dwelled in her, Mary did not live on the surface. At each moment, Mary journeyed back to her heart to totally adore and surrender to God's creative action. Elizabeth wrote:

> "The Blessed Virgin pondered these things in her heart" (see Lk 2:19, 51) . . . Her whole history can be summed up in these few words; she lived in her heart at such depths that no human eye could follow her.[60]

For Elizabeth, Mary's life summed up the entire attitude of a contemplative soul:

> The attitude of the Blessed Virgin during the months between the Annunciation and the Nativity is a model for interior souls, for those chosen by God to live "within," in the depths of the bottomless abyss. In what peace and recollection Mary kept herself ready for all things! How the most trivial events were divinized by her, for through everything the Blessed Virgin remained in adoration before the gift of God. This did not prevent her from devoting herself

externally to the exercise of charity; the Gospel tells us that Mary traveled in haste through the mountains of Judea to be with her cousin Elizabeth ([see] Lk 1:39). The indescribable vision that she contemplated in herself never diminished her exterior charity.[61]

Mary identified herself so much with Christ that she even adopted his prayer. Elizabeth once described Mary's prayer: "Like [the Word of God] her prayer was always this: *Ecce*! Here I am!—Who? The servant of the Lord, the lowliest of his creatures, she, his mother!"[62] We can see an interesting parallel between the words the Apostle Paul puts on the lips of Christ: "I have come to do your will, O God" (Heb 10:7), and Mary's response at the Annunciation: "Here I am, the servant of the Lord, let it be with me according to your word" (Lk 1:38). Both responses reflect the same attitude: a loving availability to God's will. As the dialogue of the Annunciation shows, Mary's search for God's will was fulfilled in faith. The Blessed Virgin always tried to discern God's plan for her through events. In this sense, she was truly the faithful Virgin and the model for people of prayer, for whom faith is constant communion with God's will.

In Elizabeth's last illness, she also found the Blessed Virgin at the foot of the cross. She understood that Christ is no longer able to suffer for humanity and that he desires to continue his passion in us. So with Mary as her model, Elizabeth generously offered to suffer for the Church at the foot of the cross. The Blessed Virgin revealed to Elizabeth the secret power of redemptive suffering that would complete her purification and make her Christlike. Elizabeth wrote:

> She is there at the foot of the cross, standing in strength and courage; and my Master tells me: *Ecce Mater tua*.[63] He gives her to me to be my Mother! And now that he has returned to the Father, he has substituted me in his place on the Cross so that I may suffer in myself what is lacking in his Passion for his body that is the Church (see Col 1:24). The Blessed Virgin is still there to teach me to suffer like him, to tell me, to make me hear these last songs of her soul that none other but she, his Mother, could be heard singing.[64]

## CHAPTER FOUR

# Purification in Prayer

The Divine life infused in us on the day of our Baptism is not a static, limited reality. Rather, within each person, the grace of Baptism is meant to develop and grow. On earth, grace grows gradually in the baptized Christian. In heaven, this grace grows in glory, but no longer in intensity. We can trust that at the moment of our death we will have received from the Lord all the time necessary to internalize and live our baptismal grace, which will flourish in the light of glory. The elect in heaven will have the degree of glory that corresponds to the degree of grace they have internalized on earth.

The baptized hope to see God face to face immediately after death — our logical end, as grace is meant to lead us to glory. However, many souls are not immediately admitted to the beatific vision because they failed to respond fully to

God's call during their earthly journey. In other words, they did not internalize their baptismal grace totally, or as one anonymous author put it, "they wandered on the surface of their being and did not have access to their depths."[1] Before contemplating God face to face, we must accomplish the work of internalization—and this is the purpose of purgatory. The souls of the righteous are held back in purgatory only through their own fault. There, they can no longer merit an increase in grace.[2]

Purgatory does not clothe us with grace, but purifies us from sin. So we must distinguish between a state where, despite being in grace, a person is still not fully balanced, harmonious, and subjected to moral law; and a state that results from the way a person has believed, hoped, loved, and struggled against sin.[3] God is the sole judge of our moral and spiritual responsibility. However, the trial of purgatory is aimed more at the second state. When a person did not become involved in an authentic spiritual combat, sin has left aftereffects that need to be purified. This purification is the work of purgatory in the afterlife and of active and passive purification in this life.

The saints show fidelity to grace to such a heroic degree that by the time they have reached the moment of their death, the divine life had entirely clothed their being. "The work of holiness [in the lives of the saints] was the slow labor of an 'incarnation' of grace: it is consummate when God has touched the ultimate depths of their nature."[4] According to the internal law of the life of grace, a total recasting has occurred in their being; they have allowed themselves to be fully penetrated by the divine life. Passive and active purifications remove any obstacles to the growth of grace in us. Unlike purgatory, which is borne without earning any merit, the sufferings that precede the death of the saints become sources of merit. And these purifications are normative in the life of an authentic Christian, since we all are called to holiness and to grow as fully as possible in the life of the grace received in Baptism.

## Doctrine of Grace

Before delving into grace in Elizabeth's life, let's briefly explore the doctrine of the Church concerning grace. This will enable us to learn more about the spirituality of grace and to determine the ideal psychological conditions for this "incarnation" of grace that can occur through purification.

The Council of Trent declared that we are renewed in our most intimate self in the sacrament of Baptism: "Not only are we considered just, but we are truly called just and we are just, each one receiving within himself his own justice."[5] Therefore, in Baptism we receive something new, a real justice[6] that we call grace. At the same time, the virtues of faith, hope, and charity are infused in us: "In the very act of justification, together with the remission of sins, man receives through Jesus Christ, into whom he is inserted, the gifts of faith, hope, and charity, all infused at the same time"[7] through Jesus Christ in whom he is inserted. Of course, Baptism does not eliminate the tendency to sin; a source of sin still remains in the baptized person, and the Christian must combat that tendency. More precisely, Baptism graces a person's soul, but the Christian has to cooperate with that grace so that it may imbue his or her entire being. As the *Catechism of the Catholic Church* teaches us, "Baptism not only purifies from all sins, but also makes the neophyte 'a new creature,' an adopted son of God, who has become a 'partaker of the divine nature,' member of Christ and co-heir with him, and a temple of the Holy Spirit" (no. 1265).

## Asceticism

At this point, spiritual theology teaches us that we have to collaborate in our divinization by means of an appropriate asceticism. Original sin has weakened our senses and faculties. Instead of being subject to reason, our senses often revolt, seek satisfaction, and covet goods in a way that is opposed to reason. With the help of God's grace, we can patiently and perseveringly discipline our senses in order to subject them to reason. Grace pursues this work, which not only helps us to control the appetites of our external senses, but also to discipline our imagination and memory. Our imagination especially must be weaned from curiosity and indulging in useless pursuits in order to become the humble servant of our superior faculties. Our senses, thirsty for new impressions, will have to become detached from these loves.

Once the senses have been pacified, another work of purification begins. Original sin entered humanity and created disorder and anarchy in the mind through the disobedience of reason. Grace, therefore, must penetrate the faculties of the mind to reestablish harmony. The theological virtues of faith and charity, infused with grace at the time of Baptism, will help in this process. Our intelligence often views events and people in a merely human perspective, making it unable to judge anything with the eye of Christ. Faith imbues our intelligence and fixes our gaze in the gaze of Christ. Our will is often intermingled with egoism, impurity, and self-love, which makes it unable to love God as we should. For this reason, Christ gives us his own heart with which to love the Father and our neighbor; only then are our hearts pure and detached.

Purity of the senses and purity of mind are the two primary conditions for our divinization. We must be determined to lose everything in order to be united with God. We see this in the three short parables in the Gospel of Matthew: that of the treasure, the pearl, and the fishing net (see Mt 13:44–50). In order to possess the treasure of divine life, we have to be determined to lose and sacrifice everything. In the same way, we should mistrust our attachments that may appear insignificant. Our little infidelities and our turning away from God are still very important because they prevent the Lord from filling us completely with his grace. By our attachments, even small ones, we limit God's action in us because they create obstacles to our spiritual growth.

## Methods and Result of Purification

Because we are burdened with sin, we cannot renew our being on our own: *Indeed, I was born guilty, a sinner when my mother conceived me* (Ps 51:5). To recover purity, we have to travel in reverse the route of our First Parents in Eden. We have to accept that only God can undo the web of sin in our hearts. We merely have to become aware of our sin and to make our own the cry of the psalmist: *Create in me a clean heart, O God, and put a new and right spirit within me* (Ps 51:10). Then, when the Lord sees our desire, he will make us pass through a crucible of trials, as gold is purified in a crucible of fire (see 1 Pt 1:7).

This work of purification proceeds in two phases: active and passive. However, these two phases of the spiritual life are not clearly separated. More accurately, God takes charge of our purification but he also sometimes leaves room for greater initiative on our part in the first phases of conversion. However, when we discover the depth of our radical poverty and of the sin inscribed on our hearts, we realize that we cannot remove it on our own. Furthermore, we soon realize just how much our life is interwoven with sin. At this point, we place ourselves completely in the hands of God, asking him to be our justice and holiness. This painful interior renewal requires arduous work, but it is necessary to attain transforming union with God.

God helps us to enter the desert a little at a time. He severs us from all that is not of him and removes all human supports. This may sound radical, but, as seen earlier, the love of God is a consuming fire that destroys and burns. Everything that impedes our union with God must disappear. We are remade in the crucible of suffering when all of our impurities rise to the surface and we understand the depths of our sin. We must experience this in order to be clothed in the purity and holiness of God. Though the soul feels this suffering deeply, it also knows this is the unavoidable condition for authentic love of God. A feeling of profound union with God often accompanies this painful process of purification. While we suffer, we know that God loves us. This causes deep joy in the midst of great suffering. The depth of suffering is all the greater when the process of purification is extensive and profound. The fourteenth-century German mystic and preacher, Johannes Tauler, compared this process of purification to an area that needs to be cleaned and leveled with a crude wooden broom to prepare it for threshing grain. Tauler points out that these trials can be of different intensities according to a person's temperament: "When the area is smoother, all you need to clean is a feather duster. Thus, there are some people whose soul is leveled and surrendered, and their souls are swept clean without any difficulty."[8] Active work to accept purification of the soul is needed to reach this point. The more obstacles removed, the greater the beauty. We need great patience to bear these trials without complaining and to trust that God is at work in us. In this midst of this kind of purification, we cannot pacify our own heart. We cannot seek consolation in anything but God. Total trust and surrender to God are required.

Purification can take different forms according to a person's personality and vocation. But whether someone is a contemplative or an active person, one thing is certain: we cannot reach a life of total union with God without going through a purification of the senses and mind. In contemplative souls, this purification often occurs in the realm of spiritual affectivity—since this is where the joys of union occur. For those active in the world it occurs more in their actions, which must be purified in motivation. The faith and charity of an apostle in the world is often purified through an inevitable series of failures and successes in their work for the Lord.

Tauler says purification of the soul involves:

1. The daily cross, which is not small, of disciplining all our exterior and interior activities.
2. The suffering of an ever-growing and insatiable desire for progress in holiness and charity, which grows the more we respond to grace.
3. The disappointment we feel, although trustful, due to the many failings of our poor will.
4. An anguish for lost souls similar to the one Our Lord had in the Garden of Gethsemane.
5. Exterior trials, illnesses, infirmities, loss of possessions, lack of success, opposition from fine people, etc., that must help us to attain complete detachment from all created goods.

6. Finally, painful doubts sometimes about the quality of our state of soul. . . . Temptations against faith may occur, along with lustful obsessions of the imagination, but some holy souls are spared these temptations.[9]

We should also add patient perseverance in a spirit of faith, as well as the trials and vexations of daily life. The best cross for us to bear is always the one God sends for our purification.

## Elizabeth's Dark Night

Toward the end of her postulancy, Elizabeth began to feel the crucifying trials of the different nights of the soul described by John of the Cross. First, they took the form of anxieties and painful trials of the mind; her imagination was especially troubled by strange images. Given that her contemplative vocation strongly involved using her mind and will, the trials affected those two faculties in particular, inasmuch as these were given over to prayer. Until then, she had experienced profound joys in prayer, savoring a felt union with God. But the Lord began to wean her from these consolations in order to totally detach her from herself so that she might grow in faith. During October 1902, Elizabeth attended a retreat preached by Father Vallée. The *Souvenirs* relates her experience:

> She found in [the retreat] only an increase of suffering; it was impossible for her to return to things that she had previously enjoyed in prayer. The teachings that she had

received with indescribable joy in her first encounter with the eminent priest only now seemed to increase the darkness of her trying night, so much so that those eight days were a true agony.[10]

Elizabeth began to realize that she had to undergo a profound transformation that she could not initiate. The *Souvenirs* tells us that until then,

> she had triumphed over all difficulties through the efforts of her willpower as well as through the graces of contemplation.... In this school of trials, Elizabeth rapidly began to acquire a greater self-knowledge that was to perfect her humility. God was using temptation to shed light on the abyss of her nothingness and assure her of his own glory in this soul, which he wanted to shower with the riches of his graces.[11]

She had to surrender completely to God the slow work of interior reform that she had begun some years before.[12] Only God can bring about the purification of human nature. For this reason, trials must reach the complete depths of the soul. Passive purification precedes this transforming union. In spite of the turmoil that she experienced in her imagination and senses, she remained interiorly calm and recollected. She did not identify with her suffering but rather contemplated it from a distance and in the light of faith. No one around her seemed to have suspected her intimate suffering. Even though Elizabeth's purification touched her prayer, nonetheless, relates her prioress,

> her hours in prayer would generally bring peace to the novice, even if they did not offer any consolation. But her

contemplative prayer, which was so simple, became more profound through her increase of faith. She remained like a small child in the arms of the One she loved though she did not sense him, in whom she believed without seeing, and whose love remained her assurance, even if she experienced only the rigors of his divine purification.[13]

Elizabeth allowed the Lord to prune away the useless branches of her life so that his divine life might inundate her entirely. She knew that she had to decrease in order to allow Christ to live in her (see Gal 2:20). The Lord did not spare his beloved; he would purify her in the areas dearest to her: in her faith and charity. To do this he made her aware of her nothingness, her misery, and her poverty. She began to realize that her heart could not love God as he was asking her to love, but her heart would have to be consumed so that Christ might give her his own Heart with which to love. She was finally living her definition of prayer: the union of the one who is not, with the One who is. One year after her entrance into the convent, in a letter to a friend, Elizabeth requested:

> Ask God that I may live fully my life as a Carmelite, as one betrothed to Christ. This presupposes such a profound union. Why has he loved me so much? I feel so small, so full of misery; but I love him, that is all I know how to do. I love him with his own love; it is a two-way flow between He who is and she who is not.[14]

Having read John of the Cross and Teresa of Ávila, Elizabeth was familiar with the kind of trials experienced by souls yearning to be united to God. But she was also blessed to find true spiritual guides in her superiors; their advice and affection helped her to bear her trials with patience. Not everyone has guides as skilled as Elizabeth's, and, unfortunately, many stagnate in their spiritual life due to a lack of wise and sensible advice. Once Elizabeth had some experience in these dark trials, she was able to strengthen others in their spiritual combats. Her advice is valuable since it comes from her personal experience. For instance, to a person suffering interiorly Elizabeth offered her secrets of peace, self-detachment, and self-forgetfulness. Elizabeth tried to explain God's plans by describing how he purifies souls:

> In these painful times when you feel an appalling void, think of how he is creating a greater capacity to receive him in your soul, that is, in some way, as infinite as himself. Try then to have the will to be happy in the hands that are crucifying you. I would even say, see each suffering as a proof of love coming directly from God who wants to unite you to himself.[15]

Elizabeth also describes the best attitude to have when we experience purification: to forget ourselves and remain peacefully in the hand of the One who is working on us. We can also unite our agony to that of Jesus in the Garden of Gethsemane. As always, she advises us not to remain at the level of suffering, but to find refuge in the center of ourselves where God dwells:

> I will tell you my secret: think of God who dwells in you, for whom you are a temple: Saint Paul speaks in this way, we can believe him. Little by little, the soul becomes used to living in his sweet company. It understands that it bears in

itself a small heaven where the God of love has pitched his dwelling place. Then she breathes, so to speak, as in a divine atmosphere: I will even say that there is no longer any more of her on earth than her body, her soul dwelling beyond the veils, in the One who is the Unchangeable.[16]

Elizabeth's painful purifications conformed her to the death and resurrection of Jesus Christ, which enabled her to grow in spiritual maturity. All that was imperfect in her disappeared and her soul overflowed with profound joy. She no longer felt merely human peace and joy, like the emotions of consolation at the level of the senses. Rather, she felt the very joy of God in her love for him and conformity to his will.

It is important to bear in mind that peacefulness of soul is the fruit of the Holy Spirit and the result of profound transformation through purifying sufferings. The intensity of Elizabeth's sufferings and her generosity in bearing them brought on swift purification. Regardless of the length of our purification, it is essential never to lose faith and always to believe in love. Elizabeth insisted on this love that transforms all suffering and immerses us in gratitude. She once wrote to her sister Guite, "Always believe in love. If you have to suffer, believe it is because you are loved; always love and sing a song of thanksgiving."[17]

After all the trials Elizabeth endured, we might think she would be spared as she neared the end of her life. However, another Calvary awaited her. She was to experience very painful physical suffering that undermined her health and kept her nailed to the cross with Jesus. One day, she wrote: "This illness seems a bit mysterious to me, I call it the illness of love," and again: "There are exchanges of love that are made only on the cross."[18] Meanwhile, Elizabeth's soul was being truly and totally purified. Her sufferings were now redemptive and apostolic. While she was suffering, she no longer had the impression of being distant from God; she sensed that she was in communion with the suffering of Christ who saved the world on the Cross. She wrote, "Never has my happiness been as great as when God deigned to associate me with the Divine Master's suffering." And to her mother she wrote:

> I understand better today how much God loves us when he gives us trials. You fear that I may be a victim destined to suffer; I beg you, do not be sad about that, it would be so beautiful! I feel unworthy of it! Think what it would be like to share the suffering of my crucified spouse, to go to my passion with him, to share in his work of redemption.[19]

God called Elizabeth to share the sufferings of Christ and, to some extent, experience his passion all over again. In her there coexisted the most acute suffering and the joy of knowing that she was united to the Father in fulfilling his holy will.

Sufferings, temptations, and tests are the purifying trials that both beginners and sinners experience, but contemplative souls can also undertake them voluntarily to help others. A contemplative soul can offer her sufferings for the sake of other souls, such as sinners or beginners, who need purification (see Col 1:24). Thérèse of Lisieux, for example, experienced this toward the end of her life. She willingly agreed to sit at the table of sinners to obtain the grace of faith for them. Thérèse wrote in her autobiography, *Story of a Soul*:

> Lord, your child has understood that you are the Light Divine. She asks you forgiveness for her unbelieving brethren. She agrees to eat the bread of sorrow for as long as you wish. For love of you, she will sit at this table of bitterness at which poor sinners eat and will not rise until the day you give a sign. Can she not say in her name and in that of her brethren: "God, be merciful to me, a sinner!" (Lk 18:13). Oh! Lord, send us away justified. May all those who are not enlightened by the shining torch of faith see it shine at last. O Jesus, if the table which they tainted can be purified by a soul that loves you, I am ready to remain there alone and to eat the bread of tears until it pleases you to introduce me into your kingdom of light.[20]

Saint Marie of the Incarnation[21] is another example of someone who offered herself in this spirit; in her case she prayed for the soul of her son.

Elizabeth felt that she had been chosen as one of those souls who willingly undertake trials to help others. She once wrote to her mother:

> The Master has deigned to choose your daughter ... to associate her with his great work of redemption; may he suffer in her as an extension of his Passion. The Bride belongs to the bridegroom; mine has taken me; he wants me to be an extended humanity for him in which he may still suffer for the Glory of his Father, to help with the needs of his Church.[22]

Witnessing the physical pains Elizabeth bore before her death, her sisters understood how much her childhood offering of herself for the sins of the world had been accepted.

Purifying and redemptive suffering are two realities that exist in a dialectic movement. We do not have to be totally purified in order to participate with Christ in the salvation of the world. Only in the grace of Christ, while being purified, may we obtain graces of conversion for the people around us. What matters here is the degree of generosity and love that drives us to accept God's will. Suffering has no value in itself, but it draws all its purifying and apostolic fruitfulness from the impulse of love rooted in our hearts.

Toward the end of 1906, Elizabeth felt her approaching death. She no longer had only a desire to suffer in order to be purified, but her love drove her to become more like the crucified Jesus. She confided to one of her sisters: "I no longer aspire to arrive in heaven pure as an angel, but transformed into the crucified Jesus."[23] She had reached the highest degree of love that brings about configuration with the Divine Master. Of course, it is important to realize that Elizabeth did not love suffering for its own sake. Rather, she said, "I love it because it makes me like the One who is my spouse and my love."[24] We find the same desire in her spiritual father, John of the Cross. One day, Christ appeared to him and asked him what reward he wanted to receive for a whole life of love spent in God's service, and the saint replied: "To suffer and be reviled for love of you."

Christ could live his mystery of the agony at Gethsemane within Elizabeth because her soul had such great capacities for love. No other desire was greater for Elizabeth; nothing else mattered but Jesus and Jesus alone:

> If Our Lord offered me the choice between death in ecstasy and the surrender of Calvary, I would prefer Calvary, not for the merit, but to glorify and to be like Christ. . . . If I had died in the past in my previous state of soul, it would have been too sweet! I am living in pure faith, I prefer that: thus I am more like my Master, and more in truth.[25]

Elizabeth's last days alternated between physical sufferings and periods of calm. Her facial expression, however, revealed a profound change: the darkness that had surrounded her had yielded to light. Her sufferings and trials can be explained by her great desire to live united to the Blessed Trinity and for the expansion of God's Kingdom in the world. Such precious sufferings are found only in the lives of saints.[26]

CHAPTER FIVE

# The Christian Call to Intimacy with God

Elizabeth's message of prayer remains important today because of the link she makes between the stages of the spiritual journey[1] and prayer. For her prayer is the breath of divine life breathed into us in Baptism. In this sense, we can say that Elizabeth's writings are just as much an initiation to the spiritual life as to contemplative prayer.

Elizabeth's message can help modern Christians. By developing her baptismal grace in of the midst of contemplative life, Elizabeth helps us to grasp the central reality of the Christian life. As Father Pierre de la Croix notes: "God dwells in us and we must remain before his presence within us. This reality of the presence of the Lord is the central truth of the entire spiritual life."[2] Elizabeth urges the Christian to consciously internalize God's presence in prayer so it becomes a reality experienced and made beneficial throughout the day.

Elizabeth's writings reveal that contemplative prayer is not merely a privilege of monks, contemplative nuns, priests, and religious. Every Christian is called through Baptism to grow in friendship with God, and this growth happens especially in prayer. We need to set aside times of prayer if we want the divine life to grow and radiate around us, if we want to become an apostolic and missionary soul in the Church. In ever-increasing numbers, men and women are taking seriously their responsibilities as Christians in the family, professional, social, and apostolic spheres. Immersed in the world, many people are discovering that contemplative prayer is vital and necessary. They know that they cannot collaborate with God's action in the events of history if they have not generously agreed to contemplate God in silent prayer. The person who does not live from God's presence within cannot claim to share God's life with others.

Elizabeth offers an answer to the anguish of the modern person who desires a life of prayer. For her, specific methods have little importance—prayer is born from an interior attitude of communion and intimacy with God present within us. It does not impede the hearts' spontaneous desire to express feelings that are beyond words. In this sense, anyone can imitate and practice Elizabeth's approach to prayer. Whatever we do and wherever we are, we can always recollect ourselves in our innermost self in order to pray with Christ in us. Elizabeth teaches us how to cultivate an attitude that keeps us in constant loving adoration of the Lord.

While we may not perfectly imitate Elizabeth's way of life, we can try to live in the spirit of her highly effective approach to prayer. For her, prayer is not improvisation or pious daydreaming with no real profit. Anyone who wants to commit to her way of prayer must be open to entering into the mystery of the death and resurrection of Christ. As she wrote in her "Last Retreat": "The soul that wants to serve God day and night . . . must be resolved to fully share its Master's passion."[3]

Elizabeth wants to help us to pray continually, but she never intends for us to remove ourselves from the everyday tasks of our state in life. In this sense, her model of prayer is within everyone's reach, even those most involved in apostolic and temporal work. To live this way of prayer requires only that we live minute by minute according to the will of God, who is hidden in the present moment. Elizabeth emphasizes that we can live in the presence of God only if we are sometimes willing to pull ourselves away from our activities and devote ourselves to periods of intense prayer. Elizabeth lived a heroic fidelity to daily contemplative prayer, even during great trials, and her desire for prayer is a beautiful model for us all.

Another encouraging aspect of Elizabeth's prayer is the absence of extraordinary phenomena in her contemplative prayer. Her prayer life was one of simple faith and love. Her great love for God and for others was proof of her prayer life's authenticity. To assess the quality of our prayer, we can always refer to these two signs given to us by Our Lord:

1. "Those who love me will keep my word" (Jn 14:23).
2. "By this everyone will know that you are my disciples, if you have love for one another" (Jn 13:35).

The first sign is present when we fulfill the Lord's will as manifested in the commandments and in the Holy Spirit's inspirations throughout the day. The second sign is present when we show love to our brothers and sisters around us—the true criterion and touchstone of all authentic prayer.

We need very high standards for ourselves when it comes to loving others, for that is the condition for true union with God. We can find the strength to spread love around us in prayer, and carefully ensure that our words are not critical and bitter. We should avoid indulging in the slightest slander and never hold a grudge against those who have hurt us while always attempting to take the first step toward peace. In summary, our charity and thoughtfulness should testify to God's love—especially for sinners, the lowly, and the poor. Finally, in addition to these two signs of an authentic prayer life, we could add a third: humility that comes from knowledge of God's greatness and holiness. Elizabeth can help us to come out of ourselves and to become more humble. She once wrote: "My mission will be to draw souls by helping them to come out of themselves and adhere to God."[4]

More than a century has elapsed since Elizabeth's death, but her words and message continue to answer the needs of people today. Chosen by the Lord to teach us about the value of a life hidden in God, Elizabeth can obtain graces for us in prayer. We can ask her for these graces and be faithful to her simple teaching. Today, perhaps in a way she never imagined, Elizabeth says to us the words she wrote to her mother on August 2, 1906:

> Ah, I wish I could tell all souls what a source of strength, peace, and happiness they would find if only they would agree to live in intimacy with God.[5]

# APPENDIX

# Prayers to the Holy Spirit

## Veni, Creator Spiritus

Veni, creator Spiritus
mentes tuorum visita,
imple superna gratia,
quae tu creasti pectora.

Qui diceris Paraclitus,
altissimi donum Dei,
fons vivus, ignis, caritas
et spiritalis unctio.

Tu septiformis munere,
digitus paternae dexterae

tu rite promissum Patris
sermone ditans guttura.

Accende lumen sensibus,
infunde amorem cordibus,
infirma nostri corporis,
virtute firmans perpeti.

Hostem repellas longius
pacemque dones protinus;
ductore sic te praevio
vitemus omne noxium.

Per te sciamus da Patrem
noscamus atque Filium,
te utriusque Spiritum
credamus omni tempore.

Deo Patri sit gloria,
et Filio qui a mortuis
Surrexit, ac Paraclito,
in saeculorum saecula.
Amen.

# O Spirit and our Creator,

O Spirit and our Creator,
Come and dwell in every soul you have made.
Bring to birth the flame of love
in these hearts which belong to you.

You are our consoler and our certain hope.
You are the gift of God Most High.
You are the source of our life and the fire of love,
anointing sent us from above.

You are the reflection of the Father's love,
the fulfillment of his promise, too.
You stir in us the gift of grace,
putting your wisdom upon our lips.

Your seven gifts give to your flock.
Come, fill our hearts with your own love.
You are our everlasting joy.
You are the power which can never fail.

From danger save us, Mighty One.
And help us follow Christ the Son.
Through darkness, pain and through every loss
our hope is certain, trusting in you.

Most Holy Trinity on high—
The Father, Son and Spirit one—
your people praise you with all their heart,
longing for heaven, O vision blest! Amen.

## Veni, Sancte Spiritus

Veni, Sancte Spiritus,
et emitte caelitus
lucis tuae radium.

Veni, pater pauperum,
veni, dator munerum
veni, lumen cordium.

Consolator optime,
dulcis hospes animae,
dulce refrigerium.

In labore requies,
in aestu temperies
in fletu solatium.

O lux beatissima,
reple cordis intima
tuorum fidelium.

Sine tuo numine,
nihil est in homine,
nihil est innoxium.

Lava quod est sordidum,
riga quod est aridum,
sana quod est saucium.

Flecte quod est rigidum,
fove quod est frigidum,
rege quod est devium.

Da tuis fidelibus,
in te confidentibus,
sacrum septenarium.

Da virtutis meritum,
da salutis exitum,
da perenne gaudium,
Amen, Alleluia.

## Come, Holy Spirit

Come, Holy Spirit, come
from your celestial home.
Send forth the radiance of your light.

Come, Father of the poor!
Come with gifts that endure.
Come, light of every heart.

Greatest comforter of all.
Sweetest guest of the soul.
Sweet refreshment here below.

In labor, you are comfort sweet,
pleasant coolness in the heat,
solace from our tears.

O blessed Light divine,
Visit these hearts of thine;
Fill our inmost being.

Without you, Spirit, and your grace
nothing pure in us will stay.
Any good is turned to ill.

What is soiled, make it pure.
What is wounded, work a cure.
Wash away our guilt.

Gently bend the rigid heart.
To what is frozen, your warmth impart.
Redirect our errant ways.

Fill the faithful, who confide
in your power to guard and guide,
with your sevenfold gifts.

To us, grace and mercy send.
Grant salvation at life's end.
Eternal joy, forever.
Amen. Alleluia.

# Notes

## Introduction

1. Teresa of Ávila defined mental prayer as "nothing else than an intimate friendship, a frequent heart-to-heart with him by whom we know ourselves to be loved." —Ed.

2. After Elizabeth's death, a biography with short excerpts of her writings was circulated, as is the custom for Carmelites. Her writings received such a response that Mother Germaine, the prioress of the convent, set out to write a more complete biography that would include more of her writings. This was published under the name *Souvenirs* in 1909. —Ed.

3. *La Servante de Dieu Sœur Élisabeth de la Trinité (1880–1906) Souvenirs*, Carmel de Dijon, Éditions Saint-Paul, Paris, pp. 269–270.

4. M. Philipon, O.P., *La Doctrine spirituelle de sœur Élisabeth de la Trinité*. Preface by Fr. Garrigou-Lagrange, with many unpublished documents, Paris, 1938.

5. Second Peter 1:4 speaks of becoming "participants of the divine nature." Divinization is a word that the early Church Fathers used to describe this process in which a Christian may become more like God through participation in divine grace. —Ed.

6. P. Victor de la Vierge, O.C.D., *Vie Spirituelle*, January 1960, p. 34; Prayer of Saint Thérèse of Lisieux.

7. *Souvenirs*, p. 137.

8. Elizabeth wrote this response on her postulant questionnaire when she first entered the Carmel. —Ed.

9. *Souvenirs*, p. 61.

10. Letter 169 to Canon Angles written on July 15, 1903.

## Chapter 1

1. Father Irénée Vallée was a well-respected Dominican preacher and spiritual director. Elizabeth made a retreat under him in 1902. —Ed.

2. Appreciation of Elizabeth of the Trinity by P. Vallée, *Souvenirs* Introduction, p. XLIII.

3. *Souvenirs*, pp. 66–67.

4. Ibid., p. 67.

5. M. Philipon, O.P., *La vie mystique de Sœur Élisabeth*, in "Vie Spirituelle," June 1938, p. 263.

6. This line may be based on a line from the poem "Seeking God" by Teresa of Ávila. —Ed.

7. *Souvenirs*, p. 70.

8. Ibid., p. 69.

9. Ibid., p. 79.

10. Ibid., p. 317.

11. "Élévation à la Sainte Trinité," *Souvenirs*, p. 380.

12. *Souvenirs*, p. 312.

13. Ibid., pp. 311–12.

14. M. Philipon, O.P., *La vie mystique de Sœur Élisabeth*, in "Vie Spirituelle", June 1, 1938, p. 268.

15. *Souvenirs*, p. 194.

16. Victor de la Vierge, O.C.D., Réalisme spiritual . . . , pp. 85ff.

17. J. Aubry, O.S.B., *Le Saint Esprit et notre vie spirituelle*, Fleurus, pp. 30–31.

18. *Souvenirs*, pp. 234–35.

19. This phrase is from a letter that Elizabeth wrote to Sister Marie-Odile just weeks before her death. The author quotes from it several times.—Ed.

20. *Souvenirs*, p. 237.

21. Ibid., p. 193.

22. Ibid., p. 322.

23. Ibid., p. 239.

24. Venerable Leonard Lessius (†1623) was both a moral theologian and an ascetic writer. He was a Jesuit belonging to the University of Louvain.—Ed.

25. *Souvenirs*, p. 198.

26. J. P. de la Trinité, O.C.D., *Action carmélitaine*, January 1961: "Se tenir en la présence de Dieu" (Standing in the Presence of God), pp. 1–5.

27. Letter 299 to a Carmelite novice written on July 17, 1906.

28. John of the Cross, *Living Flame of Love*, st. 1, v. 13–14.

29. Ibid., st. 39.

30. *Souvenirs*, p. 317.

31. Ibid., p. 315.

32. In the last part of her life, Elizabeth began to refer to herself by the name *Laudem Gloriae*, or "Praise of Glory," a phrase taken from the Letter to the Ephesians. —Ed.

33. *Souvenirs*, p. 248.

34. Ibid., p. 217.

35. Ibid., p. 254.

36. Elizabeth wrote this response on her postulant questionnaire when she first entered the Carmel. —Ed.

37. *Souvenirs*, p. 89.

38. See Teresa of Ávila, *The Life of Saint Teresa of Jesus*, ch. 8.7.

39. Étienne de Sainte-Marie, O.C.D., *Conversation avec Dieu*, Bruges, Beyaert, pp. 42–44.

40. Thérèse of Lisieux, *Story of a Soul*, Epilogue.

41. P. Étienne de Sainte-Marie, O.C.D., *Conversation avec Dieu*, Bruges, Beyaert, pp. 86–87.

# Chapter 2

1. "The Testimony of Cloistered Women, God Suffices," in *La Vie Spirituelle*, July 1962, p. 87.

2. A reference to what is now par. 10 in the Rule of Saint Albert given to the Carmelites by Saint Albert Avogadro in the thirteenth century. —Ed.

3. Teresa of Ávila, *The Life of Saint Teresa of Jesus*, ch. 24.7.

4. John of the Cross, *Œuvres spirituelles*, Maxime 147, Éditions du P. Lucien-Marie de Saint-Joseph, p. 1314.

5. *Souvenirs*, p. 89.

6. Ibid., pp. 269–70.

7. Ibid., p. 361.

8. The original French edition did not include a footnote for this quote. —Ed.

9. Augustine, *Confessions*, Bk X.

10. Élie de Jésus-Marie, O.C.D., *Les principes de l'oraison*, pp. 232–33.

11. John of the Cross, *Ascent of Mount Carmel*, ch. 15.5.

12. Hans Urs von Balthasar, *Élisabeth de la Trinité et sa mission*, pp. 125ff.

13. In August 1906, months before her death, Elizabeth was so ill that she was unable to join the community for their annual silent retreat. Knowing she was most likely going to die, Elizabeth prayed her retreat from her sickbed and made notes. These notes were collected under the title of "The Last Retreat." —Ed.

14. See par. 21 in the Rule of Saint Albert. —Ed.

15. Latin for "great canticle." Elizabeth is likely referring to the Canticle of Ephesians 1:3–10. —Ed.

16. Elizabeth assumes that Mary of Bethany is the same woman as Mary Magdalene, an assumption made by many of the patristic scholars but that is now sometimes disputed. —Ed.

17. Latin for "One thing necessary." Elizabeth is alluding to the passage in the Gospel of Luke when Jesus tells Martha, "There is need of only one thing" (10:42).

18. Likely a reference to Psalm 119:109: "I hold my life in my hand continually, but I do not forget your law." —Ed.

19. *Souvenirs*, pp. 343–44.

20. Ibid., pp. 362–63.

21. Ibid., p. 314.

22. Blaise Pascal wrote in his famous work *Pensées*, "If our condition were truly happy, we would not need diversion from thinking of it in order to make ourselves happy." —Ed.

23. Saint John of the Cross, quoted edition, Maxim 138, p. 1313.

24. Ibid.

25. The Taizé Community is an ecumenical Christian monastic community in France that was founded in 1940 by Brother Roger Schütz, a Reformed Protestant. Guidelines for the community's life are contained in *The Rule of Taizé* written by Brother Roger and first published in French in 1954. —Ed.

26. "Introduction to the Spiritual Retreat" in *Verbum Caro*, Taizé, no. 52, pp. 364ff.

27. Ibid.

28. See Élie de Jésus-Marie, O.C.D., op. cit.

29. This passage draws its inspiration from the "Introduction to the Spiritual Retreat," Taizé, p. 5.

30. Dionysius was a Christian theologian and philosopher of the late fifth to early sixth century.

31. *Souvenirs*, p. 362.

32. Ibid.

33. John of the Cross, *Œuvres complètes*, Éditions du P. Lucien-Marie, O.C.D., Maxim 147, p. 1314.

# Chapter 3

1. *Souvenirs*, p. 210.

2. That is, the knowledge we have of things through their appearances leads us to grasp the essence or nature of those things. —Ed.

3. *Souvenirs*, p. 18.

4. Ibid., p. 412.

5. Thérèse of Lisieux, *Story of A Soul*, Epilogue.

6. *Souvenirs*, p. 383.

7. Ibid., p. 382.

8. Romano Guardini, *Introduction à la prière*, pp. 186–88.

9. Léonce de Grandmaison, S.J., *Écrits spirituels*, pp. 192–95.

10. Thomas Aquinas, *Summa Theologiae* (II-II, q. 83, a. 14).

11. Father Jacques Loew started what is called the worker-priest movement when he began working in the docks of Marseilles, France in 1941. The movement was later repressed by Pope Pius XII. Father Loew obediently left his work at the docks but continued ministering to the working class. He was invited in 1971 by Pope Paul VI to preach the Lenten retreat in the Vatican.—Ed.

12. Jacques Loew, *Comme s'il voyait l'invisible : Un portrait de l'apôtre d'aujourd'hui*, p. 137.

13. *Souvenirs*, p. 89.

14. Ibid., pp. 88–89.

15. Ibid., p. 387.

16. Ibid., p. 50.

17. Elizabeth is referring to the pre-Vatican II arrangement of the Liturgy of the Hours. *Matins* is now the Office of Readings and can be prayed at any time and *Compline* is sometimes referred to as Night Prayer. —Ed.

18. *Souvenirs*, p. 89.

19. P. Lépargneux, O.P., *Esquisse d'une théologie de la prière*, p. 83. The author is saying that we can stop praying even if it's only because we are tired. —Ed.

20. *Souvenirs*, p. 52.

21. Ibid., p. 383.

22. Ibid., p. 416.

23. Ibid., p. 445.

24. Ibid., p. 133.

25. Ibid., pp. 52–53.

26. Ibid., p. 114, n. 1.

27. Ibid., p. 341, n. 1.

28. Ibid., pp. 218–19.

29. Ibid., p. 393.

30. Ibid., p. 47.

31. Ibid., p. 117.

32. P. Claude Geffré, O.P., *Dieu: pour quoi faire?*, in *Cahiers sur l'oraison*, no. 56, p. 332.

33. *Souvenirs*, p. 116.

34. *Souvenirs*, p. 357. She quotes Jean-Baptiste Henri Lacordaire, a famous Dominican preacher in France.—Ed.

35. Ibid., p. 167. The expression "slip under" can also be found in the writings of Thérèse of Lisieux.

36. Pères Roger et P. Dalbert, S.J., *La Méditation de l'Évangile*, no. 7, in *Supplément de la Vie Chrétienne*, no. 17, p. 35.

37. *Souvenirs*, pp. 332–33.

38. Blaise Pascal, *Pensées*, no. 172.

39. Quoist, Michel, *Réussir*, pp. 101ff.

40. R. P. Victor de la Vierge, O.C.D., *L'Instant présent* (For a Spiritual Realism), Noviciat des Carmélites, Bernay-en-Champagne (Sarthe).

41. This is a quote from Julien Green, an American writer who wrote primarily in French. —Ed.

42. *Souvenirs*, pp. 315–16.

43. P. Ranquet, O.P., *Masses ouvrières*, no. 158, pp. 16–17.

44. P. de Caussade, *L'Abandon à la Providence divine*, pp. 109–110, 22–30.

45. P. de Caussade, in *Ami du Clergé*, no. 31, August 3, 1961, XIII, Christiani.

46. *Souvenirs*, pp. 418–19.

47. See *The Christian Faith*, edited by J. Neuner, S.J., and J. Dupuis, S.J., (New York: Alba House, 1990), p. 625.

48. Thomas Aquinas, *Explanation of the Creed*.

49. 4. Sent. d. 45. qu. 2.

50. 4. Sent. d. 49. qu. 5.

51. *Doc. Cath.*, 16-9-92, no. 1384, p. 1162.

52. *Souvenirs*, p. 176.

53. Ibid., p. 391.

54. Ibid., pp. 53–54.

55. Ibid., p. 126.

56. Ibid.

57. Latin for "Heaven's Gate," an honorific name for Mary because it was through her that Christ passed from heaven to earth. —Ed.

58. *Souvenirs*, p. 374.

59. Ibid., p. 373.

60. Ibid.

61. *Souvenirs*, p. 336.

62. Ibid., p. 374.

63. Latin for "Behold your mother," the words that Jesus spoke to the beloved disciple in the Gospel of John 19:27. —Ed.

64. Ibid.

# Chapter 4

1. *Réflexions sur l'amour divin*, Carmel de Bordigné, p. 5.

2. As long as we live on earth and are in the state of sanctifying grace, God allows us to merit other graces. "The grace of the Holy Spirit can confer true merit on us, by virtue of our adoptive filiation . . . Charity is the principal source of merit in us before God" (CCC, no. 2026). —Ed.

3. In other words, in life we may not be fully integrated because we suffer from the effects of things we are not responsible for, such as traumas. The second state, instead, has to do with the effects of our own sins, which require purification. —Ed.

4. *Réflexions sur l'amour divin*, Carmel de Bordigné, p. 5.

5. *The Christian Faith*, pp. 614–615.

6. Justification means that God cleanses us of sin, and fills us with sanctifying grace. The word "justice" here refers to that ongoing state. —Ed.

7. *The Christian Faith*, p. 615.

8. Tauler, *Sermon 37, 4* (*Sermons de Tauler*, tome II, pp. 168–169) quoted by P. Hugueny, O.P., *Introd. Théol. aux œuvres de Tauler*, vol. 1, p. 153.

9. Tauler *Sermons. Int. théol.* P. Hugueny, O.P., vol. 1, pp. 152–53.

10. *Souvenirs*, p. 95.

11. Ibid., p. 97.

12. While we always need the help of God's grace, in the earlier stages of the spiritual life we must be a bit more active and take on penances to help purify ourselves. But at a certain point God has to "take over" the process by working in us the passive purifications: the dark night of the senses, and the dark night of the soul. —Ed.

13. *Souvenirs*, p. 98.

14. Ibid., p. 99.

15. Ibid., p. 100.

16. Ibid., pp. 101–102.

17. Letter 269, April 1906.

18. *Souvenirs*, pp. 176–179.

19. Ibid., p. 190.

20. Saint Thérèse of Lisieux, *Manuscrits autobiographiques*, p. 251.

21. Foundress of the Ursuline order in New France. She left her young son Claude in the care of family to join the Ursulines in France. Understandably, Claude had a difficult time when his mother entered the convent but she prayed fervently for him. The prayers must have been effective because Claude later became a Benedictine monk and mother and son often wrote letters to one another. —Ed.

22. *Souvenirs*, p. 201.

23. The praise of glory; reminiscences of Sister Elizabeth of the Trinity, a Carmelite nun of Dijon, 1901–1906 (London: Burns, Oates & Washbourne Ltd., 1912), p. 189.

24. *Souvenirs*, pp. 200–201.

25. Ibid., p. 254–55.

26. Author's Note: It could be dangerous to try to discern for ourselves if we are going through the passive purifications. We must let our spiritual director take care to discern with us the nature of the

trials, if this is useful. In this regard, we must be cautious about our own errors and vanity.

## Chapter 5

1. That is, the classic three stages of the spiritual life: purgative, illuminative, unitive. —Ed.
2. P. M. de la Croix, O.C.D., Revue "*Carmel*," 1960, p. 16.
3. *Souvenirs*, p. 350.
4. Ibid., p. 234.
5. Ibid., p. 213.

# Also by Father Jean LaFrance

### Pray to Your Father in Secret

If you want to grow in prayer, pick up this book and read it to the very end! A classic by noted author Jean Lafrance, each helpful chapter facilitates the journey to God. Your life will never be the same.

Paperback, 224 pages
Item #: 60239    9780819860231    $14.95 USD

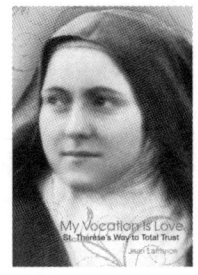

### My Vocation Is Love
*St. Thérèse's Way to Total Trust*

Find your way to total trust in God with Saint Thérèse of Lisieux as your guide. This spiritual biography includes rich commentary on Thérèse's reflections and offers glimpses into her interior life of contemplation and prayer. Lafrance captures Thérèse's growth—from accepting her own powerlessness, to placing complete confidence in God, to experiencing God's response of merciful love.

Paperback, 208 pages
Item #: 49014    9780819849014    $14.95 USD

BOOKS & MEDIA

A mission of the Daughters of St. Paul

As apostles of Jesus Christ, evangelizing today's world:

We are CALLED to holiness
by God's living Word and Eucharist.

We COMMUNICATE the Gospel message
through our lives and through all
available forms of media.

We SERVE the Church
by responding to the hopes and needs
of all people with the Word of God,
in the spirit of St. Paul.

For more information visit our website: www.pauline.org.

# BOOKS & MEDIA

The Daughters of St. Paul operate book and media centers at the following addresses. Visit, call, or write the one nearest you today, or find us at www.paulinestore.org.

**CALIFORNIA**
   3908 Sepulveda Blvd, Culver City, CA 90230   310-397-8676
   3250 Middlefield Road, Menlo Park, CA 94025   650-562-7060

**FLORIDA**
   145 S.W. 107th Avenue, Miami, FL 33174   305-559-6715

**HAWAII**
   1143 Bishop Street, Honolulu, HI 96813   808-521-2731

**ILLINOIS**
   172 North Michigan Avenue, Chicago, IL 60601   312-346-4228

**LOUISIANA**
   4403 Veterans Memorial Blvd, Metairie, LA 70006   504-887-7631

**MASSACHUSETTS**
   885 Providence Hwy, Dedham, MA 02026   781-326-5385

**MISSOURI**
   9804 Watson Road, St. Louis, MO 63126   314-965-3512

**NEW YORK**
   115 E. 29th Street, New York City, NY 10016   212-754-1110

**SOUTH CAROLINA**
   243 King Street, Charleston, SC 29401   843-577-0175

**TEXAS**
   No book center; for parish exhibits or outreach evangelization, contact: 210-569-0500, or SanAntonio@paulinemedia.com, or P.O. Box 761416, San Antonio, TX 78245

**VIRGINIA**
   1025 King Street, Alexandria, VA 22314   703-549-3806

**CANADA**
   3022 Dufferin Street, Toronto, ON M6B 3T5   416-781-9131

¡También somos su fuente para libros,
videos y música en español!